Stop, Drop, and Panic

...and Other Things Mom Taught Me

Rebecca Brown

Design by Emily Craig
Cover photo by Dejan/YouWorkForThem
Author photo by Tomas Zahumensky

ISBN-13: 978-0692689899
ISBN-10: 0692689893

This book is a love story about Mom.
She won't see it that way.

———————————————

Thank you to Dad, Ben, and Charlotte.
Without whom this book would have been one long run-on sentence.

Contents

Prologue

I'm afraid of everything and it's all my mother's fault. To be fair, she's afraid of everything and it's all her father's fault. Some people inherit family wealth or intelligence, or any number of positive qualities. Anxiety is my family inheritance.

Things that other people (read: "normal people") don't think twice about, I am terrified to do. I hesitate, agitate, hyperventilate, and ultimately avoid doing. Exhibit A: I'm now terrified of the bus.

~~~~~~~~~~~~~

I knew that night when I took my seat toward the back exit doors on the Number 16 bus that I was taking a gamble. Going home wasn't the risk; it was 10 p.m. on a Tuesday—a reasonable hour to head home for a driven, ambitious 28-year-old writer and editor living in Manhattan. Taking the bus was the problem, and sitting directly in front of the rear exit doors, despite everything Mom had taught me my whole life about being safe, was definitely life threatening.

So much so that it amped up my usual level of anxiety to new highs.

Buses, like restaurants and subway stations, had hot zones—areas in which bad things were most likely to occur. These weren't facts Mom made up from her imagination, they came directly from her father, an Italian-American born and raised in the rough and tumble depths of New York City's Hell's Kitchen in the early 20th century. "Don't look behind the car when you get in, look under the car— you'll see the killer's feet," and "Don't take the numbered streets at night, take the avenues, they have stronger street lights so it's harder to rob you," would be the first two lessons he taught Margaret Aimy Germano.

My mom.

Her dad would teach her many things like that over the course of her lifetime.

Charles Germano, born Carmine, was always on the hunt for a quick exit, be it from a neighborhood pizza joint or outdoor parking lot. He always identified the doors or escape routes closest to him before ever allowing himself to relax, although he never really relaxed.

Being present wasn't important. All that mattered was his safety and knowing where to look for the bad guys. That was how you survived in Hell's Kitchen.

They said Charles, later nicknamed Chaz, had an eidetic memory. He could remember what someone owed, borrowed, or bet just from a few seconds of being exposed to the information, which made him a particularly useful bookie. He could read or hear the details of a horse bet in his barbershop in the West Village and commit all of it to memory, all without ever leaving a paper trail. Later, when high-level bosses would come into the shop to pick up winnings, Chaz could recall the wins and losses perfectly. Down to the cent. This auditory memory was of particular importance to the most influential group in his neighborhood.

The Mob.

Mom said she never saw anyone in the Mob. She didn't remember the towering gangsters in long wool overcoats and flat-brimmed hats ever coming to the apartment looking for Charles, although one time late at night he was dumped all battered and bruised on their stoop on South 5th Street in Williamsburg, Brooklyn. No one ever mentioned what happened. Not her mom, also named Margaret, or her older sister, Suzanne. But they all knew.

It wasn't because he gave a bad hot shave.

But Mom didn't have to see the Mob to feel their presence, or to develop a fear about them lurking around every corner. When Grandpa showed her how to scan parking lots for dangerous men, or how to change course when she was being trailed, she knew, subconsciously, that somewhere — anywhere — outside of the Germano household lay danger. And it was up to her to disseminate that information to future generations.

For her, though, there ended up being a lot of danger. There was Joey "Six Fingers" Agostino, the bum that lived in their building who burgled all the apartments and, as a result, forced Charles to booby trap the windows shut every night—even during the oppressively hot and humid summer—by placing a water glass on the window sill that would crash and make noise if someone came in, and there was the creep at the Hoyt-Schermerhorn subway exit that grabbed her underwear while she walked up the stairs in a skirt.

These fears all came to a head when I was born many years later in Los Angeles, California. In the 1980s while other mothers were busy giving their six-year-old children Easy Bake Oven demos, mine was instructing me on how to fight off muggers at the upscale Santa Monica Place mall. As a result I grew up feeling loved but terrified and ready to be robbed by Joey, *et al*.

As in her childhood, preparing for a hijacking/kidnapping/mugging became as much a part of my daily routine as did brushing my teeth. I was always ready to face my attacker.

Until the day when he came. And I wasn't ready.

It was 22 years later when I found myself face-to-face with my own Joey "Six Fingers." I was living in New York, working as an editor at MTV, and riding the

Number 16 bus.

My Joey "Six Fingers" arrived in the form of a stranger, and the stranger was attempting to mug me.

Lucky me, I'd been masterfully trained for that very moment.

Lucky him, I had an anxiety disorder. So as any woman with an anxiety disorder would do, I panicked, instead.

I froze.

I might have peed my pants.

But then I put a plan into motion. Despite everything I had been taught about how to deal with thieves and deviants, I was going to ignore Mom's teachings and instead engage in a tug of war.

I was going to outsmart the Germano anxiety gene and out-muscle my thief—my independence was at stake. I was going to prove to myself that I didn't have to live my life in fear, and that I could make it in New York without Mom.

I was on a bus, at night, and I was alone. It was a tried-and-true Germano recipe for disaster.

But it didn't have to be my recipe.

I was going to fight this fucker.

Part I

Santa Monica, 1987

"There's no way we are going to see Santa this year," Mom said to me a few weeks before Christmas when I was six years old. "He's a pedophile for God's sake."

There were two words that struck me when she said that: pedophile and Santa, only one of which I knew the definition.

I was sitting at the kitchen table with Dad. I turned away from her and stared through the window at the backyard flower garden. A zippy hummingbird flew into the picture and was pecking away at the base of our red bird feeder when Mom interrupted the quiet.

"Beki, did you hear me?"

I swiveled back around and spooned a huge helping of soggy Kix cereal into my mouth, cramming in as much as I could fit, hoping that if I chewed loud enough, maybe she'd think I didn't hear her. Maybe I could choke on the Kix and that would change the topic.

Mom was staring directly at me, though, waiting for a

response or confirmation that I'd be okay with nixing a visit to Santa. But I wasn't okay with it. I was six and had seen the guy five times before, minus the one year when my Jewish father rented a plush red suit and came to our home with clumsily wrapped presents in tow. "Santa looks a lot like Daddy," I'd said to Mom that year after Saint Nick left our house. But even with the previous meet-and-greets I was sick to my stomach just thinking about missing out on Santa.

Mom was standing at the kitchen counter grinding coffee beans. I hated the smell of them. I waited until she finished and then asked, "Why can't we see him?"

She spoke up excitedly. "Well, if you paid closer attention to the newspaper story that I read to you this morning about sex criminals stalking shopping malls in holiday costumes, then you'd know what I was talking about." She poured the finely ground beans into a cone-shaped filter and hit the brew button on her Cuisinart. I tried my best to focus on what little waft of sugar I could sniff out from my bowl, but the pungent smell of coffee was overpowering.

"Oh, Samantha, will you stop it?" Dad said, rotating his wrists just enough to move the *Los Angeles Times* away from his eyes so he could rescue me from her doomsday diatribe. Dad always sat near us in the breakfast nook, but preferred to tune us out by reading the sports section. He'd been a Dodgers fan his entire life, even before he moved to

California. "Why are you terrifying her? Show me this article."

"Jack, don't do that. I already took that section of the paper out to the recycle bin."

Dad laughed and that made me feel confused. I always believed Mom over Dad because she was the holder of that type of data. She was our in-house news source and I would never question her the way he did. Plus, I was six and wouldn't have been able to read the article.

Mom shook her head at Dad when he laughed. "I'll have you know an ex-con from San Quentin State Prison is going to the Santa Monica Place mall dressed as Santa and scamming cheery holiday shoppers into giving him money," she said firmly. She delivered the information with so much authority it sounded like she was presenting a book report.

I didn't understand all the details, but when Mom said something was scary it was, so this news frightened me.

"He's taking money from innocent people, and you don't want to know what else he's doing," she went on.

I took a deep breath and held it a few seconds, listening. I did not want to get scammed by anyone (though I did not know what it meant to be scammed and I had no money anyway), so I nodded and agreed that we should not go to the mall. I'd just write the real Santa a letter about the new Nintendo games I wanted.

Mom, Dad, my half-brothers Damon and Danny, and I all lived on a strikingly beautiful street in Santa Monica. We had palm trees and perfect hedges and nary a homeless person in sight. Although certain areas of downtown Santa Monica had a homelessness problem, but not where we lived. North of Montana. A three-mile stretch near the Santa Monica Bay where property lot size doubled, apartments vanished, and kids ran around their front yards in tartan skirts and prep school blazers. A surprising number of kids in my seemingly all-Anglo neighborhood spoke Spanish, and not because their parents believed in raising their children in a bilingual household, but because moms and dads all worked as doctors, lawyers, or movie directors so they were being raised by their Spanish-speaking nannies.

Despite our impressive zip code safety rating, Mom had a unique ability to morph pedestrian events into potential catastrophes. She loved our family immensely and felt responsible for keeping us safe, so her (s)mothering campaign segued into daily discussions not only about danger lurking everywhere, but about defense strategies for even the rarest of moments. Damon and Danny were 12 and 10 years older than me, respectively, so they were spared the stranger danger talks. They were well into their teens and Mom was their step-mom; her safety seminars were easier to avoid.

Mom and Dad had both been married once before. Mom to a drummer from a Long Island-based rockband called The Vagrants—they spent the first year of their short marriage living in Haiti—and Dad to a woman he had originally met at his Jewish day camp in Los Angeles, when they were 6 and 5, respectively. Dad and his first wife had two kids: Damon and Danny. After Mom and Dad's first marriages ended, they were set up on a blind date in Los Angeles by Mom's friend Corinne.

The mother I met as a newborn and grew up fascinated by had always been tall, unfairly thin, and simply beautiful. You're supposed to say your mom's beautiful the way you're supposed to gush over someone's newborn baby. But if you saw my mom and didn't know I was related to her, you'd say, "Wow, that lady is a looker." She'd always had below-the-shoulder bleached hair that was a frothy blonde on the top and black on the bottom. She dyed it that way intentionally. She never wanted to be one of those robotic blonde ladies; she wanted people to know she was different. She dressed exceptionally hip, too. In men's slacks and big T-shirts that accentuated her slender frame. And she had a smile that could light up a room.

Mom had always gone by Samantha, and for my entire life we lived in a beautiful home in Santa Monica, except for the first three years of my life when we lived in a condo on the beach in postcard perfect Marina del Rey. She loved to cook and entertain for her family and friends, and if there was not an inordinate amount of noise coming from her kitchen, she'd blast horror films from a small TV on the counter to calm her. "Silence hurts my ears," she'd say. "All those rock concerts gave me tinnitus." Mom really did go to all those rock concerts. Her first husband the drummer, after their divorce, went on to play with Jimi Hendrix. I never believed her Jimi Hendrix claim.

But Samantha wasn't her birth name. She changed it somewhere between living in New York and driving alone cross-country to California. The mother I never met—my New York mother, if you will—was born Margaret. And according to Samantha, Margaret had it bad. Margaret was heavy growing up, a weight that through Samantha's embellished storytelling always fluctuated between 25 pounds overweight and clinical obesity. And Margaret had low self-confidence. Margaret's family was poor and lived in a dangerous part of Williamsburg, Brooklyn (pre-hipster takeover), where kids tried to drown her in a toilet bowl at school because she was Italian.

Her stories never seemed real. They felt like stories Mom told me about someone she read about in a book or saw on the television. And while Margaret upgraded her life—she moved across the country, changed her name, and carved out a great career for herself as a casting director in Hollywood before eventually meeting and marrying Dad—Samantha's always enjoyed talking about Margaret. As though Margaret were a close friend of hers from her past life.

One part of Margaret that Samantha could never let

go of was fearful, paranoid Margaret, carrier of the Germano anxiety gene. Once I was born, Samantha and Margaret put their heads together, I imagine, and figured out how they were going to keep their only daughter safe.

Even if it meant making her crazy.

"Anytime you're alone, make sure that you hold your house keys like this," Mom said to me one morning, months after we canceled our plans to see Santa. She held her giant circular metal key ring in her palm, arranging the keys so that each jagged edge popped out above her soft knuckles. Her bleached blonde rocker haircut and tinted aviator eyeglasses always made her look like a Hollywood actress to me; this time, though, she looked more like Edward Scissorhands.

It was "Learn To Use Keys As Finger-Knives" day in the Brown household, which was a big grown-up moment. I didn't have house keys because Mom picked me up from school every day, but that didn't matter; their main purpose wasn't opening locked things, it was the special way you held them in your fist when performing an uppercut key punch.

"But I don't have keys," I reminded her.

"I'll get you some. Here, now you try." I took them out of her hand and nearly fell to the floor due to their weight. They jutted out of my much smaller fingers like a bear claw. I looked at her with my big brown eyes for approval.

"Yes, Rookie. That's exactly it," she said smiling wide. I liked when Mom called me Rookie, it made me feel special.

"If you're ever nervous that someone's following you, now you can protect yourself." I thought nothing unusual about it. Surely everyone's parents were teaching them these vital life lessons. I treasured her for giving me knowledge that would ensure my safety.

In addition to her do-it-yourself brass knuckle lectures, she also explained how to properly identify predators. Most of it had to do with cars and parking lot best practices. Bad people hid in old vans at the mall waiting for someone to walk up to their car which was parked next to them, at which point they'd slide open their corroded door, jump out, and use a double-seal Ziploc to suffocate their victim. I learned how to scan parked vans for suspicious activity. When we'd return to our car together after a fun day of shopping in the Santa Monica Place mall, she'd always arrange her car keys in her fist in case anyone tried to asphyxiate us with a freezer bag. It was a good thing to practice, although I rarely did.

By age nine, I was more familiar with her canon of defense tactics than my fourth grade academic curriculum. The "Brown Household Truths" I committed to memory went something like this:

> **Grocery Store:** Typically okay, but never use the back entrance.
>
> **Parking Lots**: Hot zone. Look under the car for feet. Valet is good.
>
> **Mall:** Hide your pocketbook underneath your

clothing. (I didn't have a pocketbook, but I suppose if I did I would have put my keys in there, too.)

Public Transport: Take only as a last resort. And never sit near the exit.

Nighttime: Danger. In every direction.

Studying the five most virulent locations on Mom's list meant only thing: There was little room in my young brain to focus on anything else.

~~~~~~~~~~~~~~~~

In the spring of fifth grade I was 11 and begged my parents to let me walk to elementary school with my friend Lo. Everyone in my class was walking to school with friends, it was practically a rite of passage, and since we lived just five blocks away from school, Dad agreed that it was time. But he had to do some convincing first.

"Sam, you need to give her some space, let her try this." Dad was always on my side. He recognized early on that I needed to break away from Mom. He didn't store facts about health concerns in his brain the way Mom did, so I found it hard to believe him when he'd occasionally encourage me to ignore her. He was always reading the box scores from last night's baseball game, he couldn't possibly have scanned the police reports the way she did. So when Dad would say things like "It's okay to stand in front of the microwave" or "There wasn't a mugging outside of Big 5 Sporting Goods on Wilshire Boulevard," I doubted him. He hadn't been trained the way Mom had. Still, I wanted to do what the other kids at school were doing even though it scared me, so I silently cheered when he supported me. Though I wasn't privy to the conversation, somehow Dad convinced Mom to let me walk to school.

The morning of my big walk, I ran into the kitchen feeling jittery. I wanted to talk to Mom about whether I should go through with it, but she was busy getting Dad's food ready for work. Some unbelievably smelly chicken dish. I couldn't identify it. Knowing what I know about her now, it was probably organic, hormone- and antibiotic-free chicken parmesan made with only the stinkiest Reggiano she could find at the Italian deli. She put his entree into a reusable canvas bag along with a pre-washed apple. She always scrubbed the skin of fruit with a clean sponge the second we brought it into the house. Just in case some poor fruit-eater later forgot to wash it on their own.

The longer I waited for her to finish preparing lunch, the sicker I felt. I popped off the lid of a cereal canister and dumped in my usual serving, hoping that food would make the odd pain in my stomach go away.

Crunch.

Breakfast tasted different, though. My tongue was unusually dry, so I dropped the spoon into my bowl and watched it sink, eventually submerging underneath the organic skim milk. I felt awful.

"Mommmm," I said loudly from the table. "I'm nauseous. Maybe I should stay home today."

She looked at me and walked over. "Honey, you will be fine, I promise."

"I don't want to do this. I don't want to walk to school, it was a dumb idea."

"Stand up, Rookie," she said before hugging me. I was already five feet eight inches tall and we'd been nearly the same height since I was in fourth grade, but it felt good anytime she wrapped her arms around me. She always smelled like gardenias.

Mom let me go and walked to the coat closet to grab her key ring. "Take these just in case." She placed her key ring into my hand as though it were a Fabergé egg and almost as soon as she did that my nausea vanished.

I curled my fingers around the keys and squeezed tight. I gave Mom one final hug and got into Dad's car. FM 88.1 KJazz was playing on the radio, and erratic tapping sounds came through the front stereo speakers. Dad was always listening to jazz. I buckled my seatbelt and rolled down the window to get some fresh air. Two blocks later we pulled into the driveway at Lo's house. I ran to her door and rang the bell. Lo's housekeeper answered and let me in. I spun around awkwardly and waved goodbye to Dad, who had already pulled out of the driveway.

Inside, Lo was finishing her breakfast. Chocolate chip pancakes. I sat in her living room and turned on her massive television.

At 8:15 a.m. Lo and I left for our adventure. We walked side-by-side, past two-story homes and well-groomed gardens when, exactly one block south of her house, three middle-aged men in well-worn pants got out of a white pick-up truck and walked toward us.

Alarms started ringing in my head.

This was stranger danger. I was sure of it.

I looked at Lo, but she was oblivious, staring down at the sidewalk, then I looked back at the three men who were fast approaching.

"Lo," I whispered. "Those men. Their truck is dented."

"Huh? What truck?"

"The truck, over there," I said a bit louder. There was something Mom had warned me about dented trucks, but I couldn't remember what it was. My chest pounded rapidly as I saw the men get dangerously closer; I could hear my heartbeat. It sounded like jazz music. I knew I shouldn't have walked to school.

I froze and glanced down at my right hand hoping to see the keys standing erect ready for combat, but my hand was empty. I'd mindlessly slipped the keys into my Eeyore backpack while waiting for Lo to finish eating her breakfast. *We're going to get captured*, I thought. I scanned the block wanting to see a parent observing the situation, but there was no one. Just us and the three kidnappers in dirty pants.

I had to do something.

"Run!" I yelled. I immediately ran up the walkway to the closest house, jumped over the morning paper so as not to trample it, and pounded on the front door. "Help, help, please open up!" I pressed my mouth up against a window. "Please, come help us."

No one came.

Frantically, I turned around and saw Lo still standing on the sidewalk where I left her. She was holding a granola bar in her hand and looked confused, with her head tilted slightly to one side, which I took to be an indication that I was doing the right thing. I was saving us.

I cupped my hands around my mouth and shouted to her. "No one's home!"

She gave me that face that said "I can't hear you," but since it also could have been the "Save us!" face, I dug my heels into the ground and headed over to the next house, this time leaping over thorny rose bushes so that I could get to the front door faster. I pounded. I yelped. I shook my hands as though I were air-drying them and, after no one came, ran directly into the street to flag down an approaching vehicle.

The driver slowed and rolled down the window. "Can you take us to Franklin Elementary School?" I panted, unable to catch my breath. "Please!"

"Sure, I'm headed to Franklin, too. Why don't you get into my van?" the male driver said with a smile. In my trepidation I hadn't even noticed that I was running toward a van (way up on the danger list). The man put the car in park, walked around the front, and opened up the sliding door on the passenger side, where two other girls that looked our age were sitting, strapped into the middle row of seats. One girl was wearing a mermaid costume and a long, matted red wig.

We climbed into the third row and sat quietly. "Lo, your seatbelt," I whispered.

I didn't say anything else to Lo during the drive, I just closed my eyes and tried to calm down. I wanted to cry so badly, but I held it together and decided I'd wait until I saw Mom later that day to completely unravel. By the time the driver dropped us off and we walked straight into class, the back of my button-up shirt was completely soaked with sweat. Typically that would have embarrassed me, but not this time—I was so relieved that the three men didn't abduct us, I didn't care what I looked like.

When Lo and I took our seats in class she finally spoke. "Why were we running from those gardeners?"

I didn't know what to say. Lo didn't know anything about Mom's teachings, and she probably didn't know anything about spotting trucks, let alone dented ones. "It's one of the rules, Lo," I explained. "Didn't you see their dented truck?"

"What are you talking about?"

I clenched my teeth and strained my lips out wide into a flat smile. I felt sorry for Lo for not knowing anything about safety and danger. It was a good thing she had me to help her out. "My mom told me about it," I said. "It was also in the paper."

I didn't know at the time how telling a moment like walking to school actually was. How deep the dependency on Mom was becoming, and how debilitating it would later become. Soon I'd discover that I couldn't function at sleepovers, sleep-away camps, or even at sleep without running for help. I was slowly becoming reliant on the woman that vowed to keep me safe. At 11 I already believed her word as gospel—dented vans, rickety trucks, and questionable Santas were vile, after all—and I would do anything, no matter how embarrassing, to tether myself to her. Even if doing so created a scorching fear that would permeate every layer of my adulthood.

Nighttime, 1988

Around the age of seven I forgot how to sleep.

When Mom turned off the lights in my room at night, my heart would begin to thump. I'd place my hand on my chest like I was doing the Pledge of Allegiance, but the longer I held my hand over my heart, the louder the sound got. I hated being alone; I hated sleeping; I hated night. Nothing ever happened to me—both of my parents gave me round-the-clock atten-tion—but there was an inconsolable void I felt when Mom was visibly absent. She was my everything. When she tucked me in at night and disappeared from the room I would gasp for air. I would gasp for her.

By the age of eight, my fear of sleeping got so bad that I'd cry hysterically and either end up vomiting on my sheets or standing in my parents' room asking if I could sleep in between them just one more time. When Dad couldn't bear sharing his bed with his lanky daughter anymore, I'd grab the scratchy striped Hudson's Bay wool blanket from the foot of their bed and curl up with it on the carpet.

On nights when they toughened up and said that I had to get off their floor because I was too old to continue this behavior, Mom would sneak into my room and sleep with me. Her friends told her she was doing more harm by giving in to my nighttime fears, so she compromised by taking the floorspace. From the carpet, Mom would tell me stories in her calm voice. "Beki, we're at Bloomingdale's and someone gave us a thousand dollars." The only Bloomingdale's I had ever been to was in New York City when we'd go visit Mom's parents. We'd board the Hampton Jitney bus where they lived in Hampton Bays and ride two hours to get to our destination: 59th and Lexington. I loved it at Bloomingdale's, and I loved the stories Mom told me about shopping there equally as much. Mom would wait until I fell asleep before slipping out of my room.

One night when I was nine and alone shaking in bed, I heard one of my older brothers in the den. It was Damon. He was 12 years older than me and typically worked late at the YMCA, but for some reason, I almost never heard him come home. That night I did. I flung the sheets back and marched into the den. He was on the couch eating a peanut butter and jelly sandwich, hunched over, one elbow on his knee, hastily flipping through a sports magazine in between ravenous bites.

I needed a reason to be awake so I stuck my arms out

like a zombie and walked with my eyes closed. It was something Mom said I'd done before, so it didn't seem unreasonable to fake sleepwalking. I sat on the wooden-framed couch next to Damon and stared at the blank television. I just wanted to be near him.

Damon looked at me. "What are you doing out here?"

I buried my head in the seat cushion to mask my face. I couldn't believe how quickly I'd gone from terrified to silly. I was on the verge of exploding with laughter.

"Beki, what are you doing?" he asked again, licking peanut butter off of his fingers.

I rolled over to look at him, holding a small throw pillow over my mouth to hide my smile. I'd immediately entered some sort of game and was focused on maintaining my poker face.

"What are you watching?" I mumbled through the pillow, giggling.

He took another bite. "The TV's not on, Beki."

Damon got up and knocked on Mom and Dad's bedroom door with his elbow.

"I think Beki's sleepwalking or something," he told Dad.

Mom got out of bed, put her arm on my shoulder, and nudged me into my room. Then she laid down on the carpet next to my bed.

"We are gonna go shopping down 5th Avenue," she began. "And we'll be the only people shopping so we can go into any store we want."

I laid on the bed, three feet up from her, feeling full.

My crying, coughing, and pretending to sleepwalk routine lasted for many years, finally stalling in fifth grade—months after Lo and I attempted to walk to school together—when my parents brought me to see an adolescent psychologist.

Twice a week Mom dropped me off to see Dr. Sharon in Topanga Canyon, a woodsy, hippie-like area in the hills above Malibu where every house was required to have at least one macrame hanging plant holder. She was an older woman with medium length blonde hair that had gray specks on top that looked like they had been sprayed on with a paint can.

Dr. Sharon lived in a big home with lots of tropical plants (many hanging in macrame holders) and a koi fish in a pond at her front entrance.

One time Dr. Sharon asked me to tell her all about my bedroom. "You must have every toy in the world," she said excitedly.

I shook my head. "Actually, no. I don't like dolls and toys. But my parents buy me a lot of games from a store called Star Toys. My favorite is Electronic Battleship." I was good at Electronic Battleship.

"I see. Well, your room must be spectacular. Describe it to me."

I'd never even thought about my room before. I hated my room. "My walls are pink. I don't like pink. And there's a big crack in the ceiling from an earthquake."

"And your bed?"

"I have frilly white pillows that look like napkins."

Dr. Sharon wanted me to enjoy being in my bedroom. I found that concept to be dumb.

On the day that was to be our last session, Dr. Sharon handed me a shiny rock.

"You've made a lot of progress, and I'd like you to take this rock. As long as you hold it in your hand at night you won't have nightmares," she told me.

I believed her because the rock was very shiny.

Next, Dr. Sharon gave Mom some pre-sleep recommendations, one of which was to create a bedtime routine for me. So Mom introduced me to her childhood favorite, *I Love Lucy*. Mom purchased the entire multi-season box set off of a TV infomercial, and had Damon and Danny carry the TV from the den and put it onto a bench in my room. Then they hooked a VHS recorder up to it. Mom would lie on the floor next to me each night as we started the tape, but always snuck out before it ended. I'd watch her walk out and sit up, but then I'd turn around and look spellbound at the screen. The next thing I knew it was morning. Lucy, Ethel, and I had made it through another night unscathed.

Lincoln Middle School, 1995

"Mom, Colette invited me to spend the summer with her and her family in France," I said after seventh grade band practice, jumping into the back seat of Mom's red Isuzu Trooper. Mom and Dad were in the front.

Mom left her lucrative career as a Hollywood casting director when I was three, and after nine years of being a stay-at-home mom, she rejoined the workforce, setting her sights on Dad's endodontic practice. She'd recently started working with him, running the office, so they were always picking me up from school together. It was so embarrassing. Hardly anyone got picked up, let alone by both parents.

Dad was a quiet man in the office—he didn't need to know about someone's day or what they'd had for lunch in order for him to perform dental surgery. But Mom said he needed someone with a certain *je ne sais quoi* to relax unnerved patients when they came into his office for a root canal. More importantly, they both agreed that her amiable personality would be helpful in his practice.

I dropped my backpack and oboe case onto the car floor near my feet.

Mom answered quickly. "Oh no, that girl Colette is from a pretty wild family." She looked at me through her rearview mirror, waiting for a response before returning her eyes to the road.

I crossed my arms over my chest. "I knew you were going to say that. Everyone else gets to hang out after school with Colette."

"You've hardly spent any time with her. We can't send you off to another country together," Mom responded. She went on to defend her stance on Colette, but I made a point of ignoring her by scooting over to the window seat and pulling a brand new bag of Gummi Cola Bottles out of my backpack.

"Don't eat that garbage. Do you know how much good food we have at home?" she said. I defiantly slid one into my mouth and put the bag of candy back into my backpack, twisting the top firmly.

Colette was tall, unbelievably tan even for a Southern California girl, and had long brown curly hair that turned blonde at the ends from the sun. She wore white tank tops and satin padded bras that were one cup size too small so that her cleavage would pour over the top. When boys came up to her at school, she'd make it a point to jump up and down while she spoke so that her boobs jiggled, moving her head in curious patterns. I always stared at her when she did this, waiting for someone to point out that the jumping coupled with the padded bra was desperate, but they never did.

Mom never liked Colette. A month before I was invited to France, I asked if I could go over to Colette's after band practice—we both played the oboe—but Mom said no because there wasn't adequate supervision.

Mom knew—as I already did—that Colette's mom was an aromatherapist named Angela, although she introduced herself to me as a "therapist." Angela had a business near the beach, where she used herbs to treat people. Mom didn't care what Angela did for a living, it was the coming home late from work part that didn't sit well with her. Three hours without a parent in sight was three too many.

Mom and Dad parked the car in our driveway. They went directly into the kitchen to reheat dinner, and I dragged my backpack and oboe out of the back seat and tossed them on top of my bed. I eventually joined them in the kitchen.

Mom was standing at the granite-topped island holding a metal spatula, which she used to dig a piece of lasagna out of a deep roasting pan. She'd made pounds of it over the weekend. Enough to feed a dozen people. She scooped up the chilled brick of lasagna and popped it into the microwave. Then, she placed a paper towel on the top so the sauce wouldn't splatter. Most people used plastic wrap to cover food in the microwave back then, but Mom was way ahead of the curve; she had already found some study that linked microwaved plastic wrap with cancer.

Dad was mid-chew when he brought up the topic of France. "You know, I never got invited to anything like that as a kid," he began. "Even if I had, Grandma and Grandpa never would've been able to afford it."

Grandma Doris was born in Russia and landed in Ohio, where she eventually met and married my Polish-born grandfather, Sidney. He worked as a wallpaper hanger and painter in Cleveland, she as a payroll bookkeeper at May Company. So even if Dad had been invited by a promiscuous friend to go to France, Doris and Sidney never would've been able to afford to send him. Plus, they'd just fled Europe as children. Why would they want their child to go back?

Dad wiped the side of his mouth with a paper napkin. "Do you know that I lived in Copenhagen for a year after dental school?"

I shook my head, then looked at Mom.

He took another bite, then continued. "It would be good for you to get a new perspective. Get away from us. Practice sleeping out of the house."

I took a seat next to him and watched him chew. "If you and Colette brought your band instruments, I'd consider letting you go to Europe with her," he added.

I instantly agreed to that condition—after all, he didn't

say we had to actually play them.

Mom wasn't having it. "But we barely know Colette. I agree that she needs to pull away from me, but Beki just started being friends with her this year."

I let out a huge sigh.

It was true. We did barely know Colette.

There were over 400 students in my seventh grade class, and a girl named Rosa seemed to be at the center of it all. She had thick brown hair and wore so much gel that her curly strands had the consistency of Top Ramen. I stared at it in History class, entranced by each noodle. During break I asked her questions about her impeccable hair and eyebrow maintenance, so much so that she eventually said I could hang out with her at lunch near the basketball courts. I pinched myself.

I was eating an English muffin near the courts, near Rosa and all of her popular friends, when she asked me where I lived. "So, like, do you have a house or an apartment?" I wrapped up my muffin and put it into my bag. This was not a question you wanted to be asked.

"A house," I said shamefaced, angling my back away from the kids playing basketball. Rosa cocked her head to the side, one eyebrow arched higher than usual. She laughed through her nose.

"What, do you live above Montana Avenue, too?"

That was definitely not a question you wanted to be asked.

"Yes," I answered quickly.

Then she hit me with it.

"Is it big?"

I wanted to tell her no. Rosa was asking for my "cool kid credentials" and I had none. I looked toward the sky and squinted at the sun, then looked back at her in utter defeat. *What was I going to tell her*, I thought.

"It's big now," I paused. "But it used to be small. My parents remodeled it because there was mold growing inside one of the bedrooms."

I immediately judged myself for my word choice. *Who says remodeled?*

Rosa opened her mouth to laugh at me. I quickly went on about the mold. "My Mom said we could have gotten very sick from all the bacteria," I paused to think. "There was an article in the paper about bathroom fungus."

That was true.

"I had no idea you were a rich white girl," she said, with the intent to insult, and before I had a chance to even think of how I'd defend the accusation, the bell rang.

I speed-walked to history and took the very last seat in class.

Later in the day I found Colette in the band room. "Do you want to meet for lunch tomorrow?" I asked.

She smiled and said yes. Even with her stuffed bra and stupid slutty tendencies, Colette would never ask me about my house.

Friendships had been built on less.

In the Weeds, 1995

Colette found me right after the bell rang. I was walking out of my science class when she spotted me and waved. I knew exactly what she was going to ask me, and I was going to say yes.

"Do you want to smoke weed with me and Michael after school?"

I smiled.

Michael was my classmate and he was the weed guy at Lincoln Middle School.

Since the start of seventh grade, I'd heard people say that smoking weed was the coolest after-school activity. In sixth grade classmates were smoking beedis, which I understood to be thinly wrapped leaves stuffed with tobacco, but by seventh grade, beedis were old news; it was marijuana everyone wanted.

After the last bell I found Colette standing outside of the tennis courts on the eastern edge of campus. "So what's the plan?" I asked her, holding tightly onto the straps of my backpack.

"Mike is meeting us here."

Hours earlier when Colette invited me to join her and Michael, I hadn't given any thought to how we'd execute the smoking of the weed, or how we'd handle the aftermath. How would I behave after doing drugs? Did this mean I was going to be a drug addict? I needed to get these thoughts squared away. It all swirled around in my head like a tornado of doubt.

"Do you think we should really do this?" I finally asked her, hoping to trigger uncertainty she may have had about it. By then, though, I'd spotted Michael's blue spiky hair across the street and knew my window to back out was closing.

"Don't come if you're not gonna do it," she told me before gliding toward him.

I paused a second, then went after her, my voice trailing in the distance. "My mom thinks I'm going to your house, so we just can't do this for long."

I'd recently won the Colette fight with Mom. As long as I called her once I got to Colette's house, and several times during my time at Colette's house, it was okay to go. This would be the first time I lied to Mom about going to her house.

Michael greeted us with a half-hearted "What's up?"

and led us into an underground parking lot a few hundred yards away from the tennis courts. We followed him up a flight of cement stairs and into an apartment. The door read 7A. One of the screws mounting the number was missing.

Inside, Michael introduced us to two guys that looked our age named Marco and Evan. They were seated on the edge of a sagging floral couch playing a loud video game. I loved video games, just not violent ones. They gave us a silent hello with their chins when we walked inside, but continued to play. I followed Michael and Colette inside and sat on a wooden chair next to the window.

"Have you done this before?" Michael asked while pulling a joint out of his pocket. I lied and nodded my head yes. I felt confident in my nod. It was cool, like how Marco and Evan had nodded.

"Ooh, what ya got?" Marco hit the pause button on his controller and tossed it onto the carpet, where it bounced a few times before landing. He leaned forward to grab the joint, and I noticed that he was wearing navy blue corduroy slippers. The kind that wouldn't hold up outside for more than a few steps. *He must not have come from school,* I feared. Marco took a few puffs from the joint then passed it to me. *Has he been kicked out for drugs? Or worse?* There was an alternative school in Santa Monica called SMASH. When kids got kicked out of my school they went there. I wondered, since I'd never met Marco and Evan before, if they went there. To SMASH.

The joint was thin and small, and the pointy edge where I was supposed to put my lips was already wet from what I presumed to be Marco's saliva. I glanced at his corduroy slippers again. They had a permanent crease at the heel from being worn incorrectly, and the thin strip of rubber at the bottom which was really more of a design element than a utility was worn raw, right down to the fabric. *Maybe Marco wore those slippers to school,* I decided. *Yes, he's in school. Not SMASH, some other school. Private, maybe.*

I inhaled deeply, holding my breath for exactly three seconds, then let out a big, heavy hacking cough so loud I thought burning bile might come up. I tried it again and coughed even more.

"I thought you said you smoked before," Michael said to me, taking the joint away and handing it back to Marco.

Not a minute had passed before I heard someone talking directly outside of the apartment. I jumped and moved the blinds.

"She's paranoid," Colette smirked.

"No I'm not," I snapped at her. "I heard someone outside."

There were five people in what I believed to be a stranger's apartment, all smoking marijuana, and for a reason that I couldn't figure out, not one of the four was concerned about my discovery. There was someone outside, possibly listening to us. Possibly getting ready to arrest us and send us to SMASH, slippers and all.

I couldn't handle everyone's laid-back attitude—they just didn't get it—so I told Colette I had to go and immediately left. She didn't even ask me why. She just said "Okay, bye."

As soon as I shut the apartment door and saw that no one was outside, I plodded back to campus in search of the girl's restroom. My feet felt like bricks, like I'd just woken up from a deep sleep and couldn't regain my balance.

Whatever was happening to me needed to stop.

School was officially over and the restroom was empty. I quickly dispensed a mound of pink grainy soap into my hand, then pressed the tiny soap granules into my mouth, rinsing the rough suds around my tongue like a sandy mouthwash.

Scrape.

Once I gathered myself I called Mom from the school pay-phone to ask her to come get me.

"I thought you were going to Colette's?" she asked, sounding worried.

My eyes filled with tears. "She ended up going somewhere else after school, I'm not sure."

Mom didn't ask any more questions. She knew something was wrong and said she'd leave Dad's office immediately.

I had about 20 minutes before she arrived, so I went to the drugstore nearby to buy Trident gum to mask the smoke-soap residue on my tongue. When the clerk asked for money I took a short, jerky breath, threw down a five-dollar bill, and ran out of the store in search of Mom.

The Isuzu pulled up near the curb and I got into the front seat ready to collapse. Mom extended her right arm out to hold me and I threw myself into her chest, quivering.

"Mom, I'm really scared."

She turned the car off.

"I smoked weed and I feel really weird." My shoulders shook intensely as I leaned into her chest.

"How much?"

"I smoked it three times with this boy Michael and my mouth is dry and I feel shaky. Help me make it stop," I sobbed.

"This won't last long, I promise."

I stopped shaking. It was just what I needed to hear.

"I'm happy you called me," she said as she turned the car back on. "I don't care how mad you think I'll be, I always want you to call me."

The pain in my chest floated into the air and evaporated.

When we got home she told me I should take a nap and brought me a big glass of organic apple juice. "You're probably thirsty," she said.

I took a huge gulp from the cup and kept my eyes locked on her. "Thank you."

An hour into my deep snooze she knocked on my door, opening it before I even got a chance to say come in. I was disoriented.

Mom sat at the edge of my bed and put my feet on her lap. "How are you feeling?"

"Fine." I reached for the apple juice cup but it was empty.

"Good. I knew you'd be okay." She started to pet my feet as she would a lap dog. "But I'm disappointed in you. I thought I raised you to make better decisions than that."

I pulled my feet out of her lap.

"I'm not grounding you. I'm just sad. I thought you were stronger."

I gritted my teeth while she finished, tasting soap residue, then relaxed my jaw just enough so I could yell at her to leave my room. When she walked out I threw a pillow against the door and screamed into the air a loud and pathetic "ugh." I couldn't believe I had called mommy for help. I couldn't even smoke weed, how could I ever convince her that I could make it in France?

~~~~~~~~~~

The phone rang seven times before Colette's dad's answering machine picked up. "Hello, you have reached Adem, I am not here," it said in a thick and unfamiliar French accent. Mom and I were at Colette's house with her mom, Angela, having a get-together to discuss France. Adem lived in France. We were trying to reach him.

Adem's answering machine beeped at the end of the message, but Mom leaned forward in her chair and pushed the speaker button on Angela's phone to disconnect.

"I suppose he's just out again," she said.

In March of my seventh grade year, months after I'd asked Mom and Dad to go to France, they finally signed off on the summer trip. It took a lot of convincing.

The plan seemed simple. Colette, her twin sister Nicole, Nicole's friend Mollie, and I would stay with Colette and Nicole's French grandmother. Colette and Nicole were American, but their father Adem was French—and he would also be there. Safety in numbers. When Mom learned that there were four girls traveling together and a big house filled with lots of family members she calmed down.

Even with the go-ahead from Mom and Dad, I knew I needed to mitigate their impending nervousness over my leaving their watchful eye for three months, so Colette and I set up a series of meetings at her apartment in Santa Monica. That way, my parents could ask Colette's mom, Angela, questions about France, and Mom could verify with her own eyes that Colette's home was child-safe and not brimming with delinquents.

"Yeah, they're not that great about communication over there," Angela answered after we heard Adem's answering machine pick up. She then reminded us of the time differ- ence, and said it would be unlikely, given that we were so far away in California, that they'd be able to coordinate a phone call.

"That's absurd," Dad said raising his voice. "There are

far more complicated things happening in the world, I'm sure Adem can find the time to answer our call." Dad rarely spoke loudly and even though he was right, I clenched my teeth when he chimed in.

"Jack, I promise they will be fine, "Angela said, slowing her words the way people did when speaking to an elder who is hard of hearing. "I'll even send the girls with my new lavender oils."

I held my breath and looked at Mom.

"Alright, well it's time for me to get dinner ready. Thank you Angela for," she paused, "hosting us."

I climbed into the back seat of the car quietly.

"You know Beki, there's something flaky about that woman, but your mother and I believe this will be a great trip and an experience we'd never want you to miss out on," Dad said to me as we drove home. I made eye contact with him in the rearview mirror. "It will be different there than you're used to."

Then Mom chimed in. "And don't touch any of her oils."

I nodded.

I nodded because I needed France. Three months away from Mom meant I could challenge myself in a way I never had. I could test myself to see if I could sleep away from her for 90 whole days. Not just in a different room of the house, but in an entirely new country.

It would be the ultimate challenge.

I had to succeed.

Bryan, 1995

There was something about Bryan's sparkling blue eyes and perfectly straight brown hair that I found irresistible. He shuffled around middle school in baggy pants and wore a graffiti-covered black backpack high up on his back, most likely to show off how little schoolwork was inside of it. He had danger written all over his face.

I fell for him immediately.

In April of my seventh grade year a schoolmate named Megan came up to me after lunch and said that Bryan was asking people about me.

Lincoln Middle School was predominantly white, with a 20-percent Latino population, and while I didn't understand much about race and privilege at the time, I knew that the size of my house—all 4,000 square feet of it—made me an outsider, socially speaking. Rosa had made that very obvious.

The majority of kids in school, at least the so-called cool kids, lived in apartments. It wasn't cool to have money. I may have been part of the dominant demographic at Lincoln Middle School, but I felt ostracized.

I found the idea that Bryan liked me impossible. He was cool, and he lived in an apartment. Living in an apartment made him twice as cool. Plus, no one had ever asked about me in that way. I was a good six inches taller than everyone in my grade, with chubby thighs and an awkward gait that was caused by my own laughable attempts to appear shorter. And I dressed like a tomboy, with wide-leg jeans and large skateboard T-shirts that I usually stole from my older brother Danny's closet. If Bryan said I was funny, maybe I would've believed it. But pretty I was not. It had to be my new wild marijuana-smoking reputation that he found interesting, and that was good enough for me.

"No lie," Megan said when I told her I didn't believe her. "He's sprung."

Sprung was an adjective I was certainly familiar with. It's what happened when you liked someone a lot and became mildly obsessive about them. Like in the movies.

As it turned out, Bryan was friends with Michael, so the more Colette and I showed up at apartment 7A after school to get stoned, the more people at school were willing to overlook my parents' checking account and consider me friend-worthy. The more Bryan was willing to consider me sprung-worthy.

A few days after Megan told me the scoop on Bryan,

Colette and I went to smoke in an alley instead of 7A. "I found this better spot in the alley," she said. By then I'd smoked with her at least a half dozen times, so I was up for a change of scenery.

Colette led me up the adjacent alley on 15th Street, a block away from school. "It's just over there," she said pointing to a recycle dumpster.

I followed the path of her finger with my eyes, then squeaked. Behind the dumpster was Bryan, sitting on what looked like a milk crate, with his brown glistening hair swooped over his line of sight.

"Did you know he was gonna be here?" I whispered to Colette, regretting that I'd said anything to her about him. She was never one to hold a secret.

"Bryyyyyyyyyan." She screamed his name in a shrill high-pitched voice. "We sure are happy to see you," she added, forcing an exaggerated laugh out of her mouth.

I glared at her blankly. I didn't understand how that sentence and that octave was going to help me any. I'd told Colette that Megan said he was sprung, so she knew exactly what she was doing when she said his name so annoyingly. "I hate you," I muttered, still following her to the promise dumpster.

Bryan stood and took a step toward us. He ignored Colette's pathetic attempt at flirting and got straight to business. "Yo, come back here I'll show you guys what I got."

Behind the dumpster, Bryan told me and Colette about

the type of marijuana he had on him. He spoke passionately about it, explaining intricate details about the buds and its coloring, but I completely zoned out and stared at his front teeth instead—like his hair, they were perfect and straight. I wondered if he ever had braces. I still had mine and hoped that, now that he was getting a good look at me, he'd overlook my mouth of metal and remain sprung. Or blind, which would at least explain how he liked me.

He interrupted my train of thought when he whipped out a dingy plastic bag from the small compartment of his backpack. Bryan made an inaudible noise that sounded like "booyah," then waved it back and forth in our faces like a flag. I saluted him. It was weird.

There he was, with his Pacific Ocean-colored eyes, flawless dental work, and dirty sandwich bag of special marijuana. I wanted to say something to him—smile, even—but I was frozen, from the feet up.

We were inches away from each other and, according to Megan, mutually sprung. I slipped my hands into the pockets of my long overalls and squeezed my thighs hard. It was a technique I'd used occasionally when I wanted to refocus my attention on something else. It rarely ever worked, but it was worth a try.

"Let's get stoned," he said breaking the ice. Bryan pulled a glass pipe out of his Dickies painter's pants pocket, pinched a small piece of weed from the baggie, and carefully packed it into the bowl. Then he held the smooth glass up to my mouth. It felt warm on my lips.

"Hold your finger here," he said, delicately moving my pointer finger over the marbled glass hole. I closed my eyes and inhaled slowly, sucking in the marijuana and his cologne simultaneously.

I was ready to take another hit when Michael trotted over to us from the other end of the alley. "Yo, you guys need to leave. Someone called the cops again."

Cops? Again?

Michael got onto his skateboard and we ran after him, through a gated apartment walkway and into a parking lot where we were hidden from the street.

"What now?" I asked, trembling.

"We need to get out of here, but you guys can't come over," Bryan said.

I thought he might elaborate, but he didn't.

There was no way Bryan was coming to my house. Even if we weren't getting high, Mom would have lost her mind if she saw him. His clothes were enormous and she'd assume that the tagging on his backpack made him a gangbanger. She'd pat him down, make a citizen's arrest, and maybe even Mirandize him on sight. Then she'd smell him, then she'd smell me, and then it would all be over—France would be but a dream. I only had two months to go before France and I couldn't screw it up.

"Let's split up, the cops will go away eventually," Bryan instructed. "But hey, do you have a second?"

He was talking to me. He wanted a second with me.

The world disappeared and I was back staring at Bryan's perfect eyes.

"Megan told me you don't have a boyfriend," he said.

I let out a weird giggle, then answered. "Yeah, I don't have a boyfriend."

I held my breath, waiting for what might come next.

"Do you want one?" Man he was slick. "Do you wanna be my girl?"

"Yes."

For the first few weeks of our relationship we held hands mostly, meeting up after school to smoke together in apartment 7A and cuddling on the floor when we were stoned. Sometimes we'd kiss each other goodbye at the end of our group smoke sessions, but they were quick pecks on the lips followed by strangely courteous hugs.

I was five inches taller than Bryan, so I was never able to nestle against his chest the way I'd seen other couples do. To avoid the embarrassment of having Bryan nestle against my chest, which is what would have naturally happened if we accepted our obvious height disparity, I stood an arm's length away from him and stuck my butt out. By the time I curved my way back in, I was four inches shorter. None of this bothered me, though. With him I was a free woman.

With him, girls like Megan and Rosa noticed me again. That was worth any potential scoliosis I might later develop.

We were a month into our provocative holding-hands-only relationship when Bryan called me one afternoon after school.

"Yo," he shouted when I answered. He was totally high. "I'm gonna roll through with Michael. We're at his house now, but his mom is making us leave."

During the time in which we had been dating, Bryan figured out that I lived above Montana Avenue, but he didn't know my exact address. While most of the North of Montana homes were large, there were still some that were smaller and older looking, like our house before Mom and Dad tore it down and built our behemoth. Because of the mold. That house was half the size of our current one. I'd let Bryan think I lived in one of those.

"You're gonna come here?" I winced.

"Yeah, you scared I'm gonna steal something?" He laughed his James Franco laugh.

"You can't come over," I said, before eventually conceding and giving him my address.

I slammed down the phone and screamed. I calculated how long it would take them to leave Michael's apartment, cross Montana Avenue, and get to my house. Twenty minutes. That's all I had before they were going to take note of our square footage and towering ficus trees.

I looked out into our entryway. The front door was 11-feet

high and opened up into a sprawling room with unblemished walls and enough architectural books to start a library. It was intimidating. Quickly, I tossed clothing over the white stairwell to mask the modular railing, opened closet doors to make the first floor appear narrower, and left the garage door open to highlight the little bit of motor oil that once spilled out of a contractor's truck.

In the garage I tossed remnant pieces of cardboard like Frisbees, watching as they crashed into the bikes that were hanging along the wall. I wheeled the trash bins from the side of the house to the center of the driveway to create a maze-like mess, and took a seat on the curb hoping that a beat up sedan would park outside or someone would tow in a moon bounce. All cars—even dented vans from the mall—were welcome.

I picked the skin around my cuticles and stared aimlessly to the south. An hour went by before I looked down at my hands and saw that my middle finger was covered in dried blood so I went inside to rinse it off. Just then, the phone rang. It was Bryan.

There was music and screaming in the background when I answered. He went to Rosa's apartment to smoke instead. "Rosa told me you live in a really big house and that you are rich." I took a huge breath through my nose and held it like I was preparing to dive into a pool. I kept holding it. *Maybe I can just faint this away*, I hoped.

"No, no. It's not big," I exhaled.

"Don't lie, dude."

I wanted to apologize and say that I was sorry I had a big house and for leading him on to think I lived in a medium-sized one.

"Ha, you're just another rich white girl," he accused me, speaking loudly so that everyone at Rosa's could hear. Not that they needed to.

Bryan was also white, but because he lived in an apartment many important blocks south of where the massive Santa Monica homes were, he was able to say that to me and make it hurt. He said it in the same way you might tease someone when you catch them picking their nose in class, leaving them with no out except to feel stifled by shame. And I was.

I slammed the phone down and unplugged the cord from the wall in case he decided to call back.

An hour later I plugged the phone back in and jumped when it rang. I hoped it was Bryan calling to apologize.

I took a deep breath, wiped the tears away from my face, and answered.

It was Michael.

He said he had something to tell me.

"Is Bryan still there?" I asked.

"Yeah, he's here. Bryan can't talk, but he wants me to tell you that you guys are done."

I pressed the phone into my cheek, letting my wet skin stick to the receiver. Then I carried the phone over to the mirror in my room and sat down on the carpet so I could stare at myself.

I needed Bryan. Not as my boyfriend, but as someone that could validate my new identity. Who I was, was a wide-eyed pre-teen that grew up in a perpetual state of fear, believing everything and everyone was a potential threat. Who I wanted to be was the opposite of that. Someone so cool that they didn't have time to be scared. But I needed Bryan's authentic badassness by my side.

With the bedroom light off my eyes seemed tortured. I'd never been saturated in my own pain before. I looked terrible. Uglier than I'd ever seen myself.

I looked at my reflection again.

Hmm. Maybe I can be bad without him, I thought.

I popped up from the carpet and turned the light back on.

"Tell him," I paused, staring heavily at myself. "Tell him I said 'good'."

Summer of France, 1995

On July 1st after 16 hours of flying across the world, Colette, her twin sister Nicole, Nicole's best friend Mollie, and I arrived at Toulouse Blagnac International Airport in the south of France. There was a sizeable crowd of people gathered at our arrival gate, but Colette and Nicole didn't recognize anyone when we stepped off the plane.

Not a single person.

I found it strange that, with all the planning we did back in Santa Monica with my parents and Angela, we managed to land in France with no one to pick us up. It seemed like an easy enough task: find out what time the girls land, and go get them.

"He might be standing somewhere else," Colette said optimistically when we got to the gate. "I'm gonna check nearby." Then she walked away, bouncing as usual.

Nicole shook her head and picked up the payphone, which was just a few feet away. We were surrounded by bustling passengers in every direction. Squeaky duffel bags and overworked suitcases buzzed around like mosquitos. Piercingly loud announcements—albeit in French—blared throughout the building's PA system. The place was a zoo.

"Maybe one of the announcements is for us," I suggested to Nicole after hearing what could have very well been a message for us. "It could be your dad telling us he is waiting for us in a different area," I continued. "Do you understand what they are saying?"

Nicole looked at me with a dead stare, then pulled a calling card out of her wallet. I watched as she made a phone call.

"Dad?" she said, sounding baffled. "You're supposed to be here!"

My heart toppled and I nearly did too.

They spoke briefly, then she placed the slick black receiver back on the holster and turned to me. "He's going to be a little late."

My limbs went numb. "I'll call my Mom, she'll know what to do." I tossed my backpack onto the floor and knelt down next to it so that I could search for my pre-paid calling card.

Nicole let out an enormous sigh. "You need to relax. My dad will be here."

I detested when people told me to relax. It was fucking annoying, not to mention impossible for me to do. *Sorry I'm concerned that we're in a country I've never been to and no one is here to get me,* I wanted to say. I glared dramatically in her direction, then stood up and walked away to update Colette, who was still eagerly searching for her dad.

When I told her she didn't even blink.

There was nothing we could do. I had to just be patient, but I really wanted to call Mom. I wanted her to tell me we'd be fine. Or that I'd be fine. I didn't care about them.

To pass the time, Colette bought a box of hair dye from the airport beauty store. The four of us locked ourselves in a handicapped restroom so that she could color her hair jet black. She'd been wanting to color her hair anyway, she said, and this was as perfect a time as any.

"I've never had black hair before," she told us.

Colette opened the box and pulled out the contents, placing them neatly on the counter of the handicapped restroom. The instructions were in French, and since only she and Nicole understood any of it, Mollie and I stepped back and watched while the sisters poured thick globs of dye onto Colette's hair and massaged her scalp.

The drippy, slick goop sat in Colette's hair like a clump of pudding, jiggling ever so slightly anytime she spoke or laughed. For the most part, though, she was stationary, waiting the recommended 20 minutes for the dye to set, which for her was a feat—I couldn't recall a time when I'd seen Colette sit still for that long.

When time was up, she got undressed and went into the stand-up shower to rinse everything out. With the dye completely out, Mollie and I took turns shaking Colette's hair underneath a hand dryer that was mounted on the wall. We didn't have a brush handy, so I used my fingers to comb through the tangled pieces.

Colette's hair was long and thick so it took forever to dry. When we finished, she flung her tresses back with such vigor she could have easily gotten whiplash. We all looked at her through the mirror for a final evaluation. She was even prettier with black hair.

"Well, what do you guys think?" she asked with a smirk.

Nicole looked directly at her twin sister in the mirror. "It's okay."

Outside of the bathroom beauty parlor we found a table with seating near a small restaurant in the airport. A strong hint of pizza floated throughout the airport and it made me hungry.

I pulled a travel book about France out of my backpack and started thumbing through the pages. Hidden in between pages 28 and 29 was a single dollar bill with the words Lucky Buck written above George Washington's face. Mom was always sending me off with Lucky Bucks when I went on new adventures. If I was starting a new grade or trying out a new day camp, there was always a single bill hidden somewhere promising me well-wishes. I wondered what Mom would have thought about this predicament and I wished Nicole would have let me call her.

It felt like several days passed before Adem arrived at the airport. When he appeared, Colette and Nicole ran to him the way anyone would who hadn't seen their father in a long time. He gave them huge hugs, then walked over to meet me and Mollie.

Adem smelled like coconut sunscreen and was as tan as Colette. He was a tall, thin man and wore a large white tank top that slipped off his rounded shoulder when he shook my hand to say hello. The shirt looked like it was someone else's top—a much larger man's, perhaps. I wanted to ask him why he was late, but I didn't. No one did.

We followed him to a very small French car and he told us we'd have to squeeze in tight. Adem drove fast, buzzing down double lane highways and whipping up winding roads that curved in all sorts of squirrelly directions. I rolled the window down and closed my eyes, but Colette's freshly dyed hair started flying around so she asked if I could roll it up.

An hour later, Adem made a right turn onto a long and unpaved dirt driveway and shut off the engine. "We're here!" he announced. There was nothing around us but fields of brush that looked like they'd survived a fire or California drought.

I limped out of the back seat and stretched my sore limbs, reaching first to the blue sky then down to my feet.

At the far end of the driveway I spotted a dilapidated farmhouse. It had wooden shutters and at least two stories that I could see. It was sort of cute and charming, like an illustration I would have seen in a children's book. Adem brought us to a side door and down a wooden staircase to the basement level of the house. He nudged open a flimsy door and pointed to a room: our room. He said that he'd be staying on the second floor with his "concubine" and the concubine's daughter. I knew what a daughter was, not so much a concubine.

Adem had a list of rules that we had to follow that touched on things like curfew and tips on using the basement bathroom. "This bathroom is not for four people, so don't use it a lot." It was a sound tip. You could tell just from looking at it that it wasn't a sturdy toilet, and I wasn't going to question him. I didn't get the impression that these were flexible rules or that Adem was a flexible man. Even with his scrawny shoulders.

The most important rule, however, was not about curbing our bowel movements. It was that we were never allowed to enter the second floor without permission. We could ask for it, but we'd need a very convincing reason for going up there. The first floor was permissible, obviously, because that's where the television and kitchen were, but definitely not the second.

"Why can't we go up to the top floor?" I asked after he showed us to our basement and left.

"He thinks we're gonna fight with Celia and Marie, which is so stupid," Colette answered. Celia was the twins' step-sister, from Adem's first marriage. She was 16, even prettier than her two step-sisters, and had big thick hair that practically twirled on its own. No one ever mentioned Celia during our France preparations. In fact, no one mentioned Adem's new "concubine" or her daughter Marie, who was 10 years old and looked like Augustus Gloop from *Willy Wonka* but without the turtleneck sweater. Marie was short and sturdy, and hardly needed protection, but maybe there were things I didn't know.

"Is this where you normally sleep when you come here?" Mollie asked Nicole.

Nicole shook her head. "Nope."

I wanted to know where Nicole usually slept, but Mollie never asked her, so I didn't either.

The layout of the basement bedroom area was in no way fit for four pre-teenage girls. On one end was a garage with two rusting cars that probably hadn't been turned on in decades, and on the opposite side was our room, which had a flimsy wooden partition that created the illusion of bedrooms. There were old pieces of artwork on the walls that all looked identical, framed in faux gold.

The room smelled wet and familiar, like the mold from our old house in Santa Monica before we remodeled it.

Colette and I looked at the available sleeping nooks and dropped our luggage onto a pair of lumpy twin beds. The beds stood at varied heights, but they were raised off of the ground, which is certainly more than I could say for Nicole and Mollie, who got stuck with a king mattress that rested on the dank brown carpet. It was the kind of cast-off mattress you might find leaning against wet garbage bags on any New York City curb.

Nicole sighed. "I'm going to the first floor to find grandmother." Then she ran up the staircase. Colette and Mollie joined her.

I scanned the room. "I'll be up in a minute."

Curious about what else was in the room, I finished the basement tour myself. On one side, there were two small screen-less windows that looked out onto a crystal blue pool.

To the other side was a closet. Mom always had spare pajamas and nice smelling soaps on-hand for guests, so I opened the closet door to see what Grandmother had for us. A metal chain connected to a bare bulb dangled from the ceiling. I pulled on the chain to illuminate the closet, then immediately jumped back toward the door. It looked like a grocery store inside, except instead of cereal boxes and juice stacked on the shelves, there were hundreds of sealed clear glass jars, piled all the way to the top. I peered closer to see what was inside them. Animal parts. All sorts of them, from flesh-colored ears and snouts to organs I couldn't even identify.

I could feel the hair on my neck stand.

I yanked firmly on the chain, shut the door, and sprinted up the staircase to the first floor, yelling, "Where is the phone?"

Writing as a Shield, 1995

Since arriving in Toulouse, Colette and her twin sister Nicole spent every cloudless afternoon stretched out on lawn chairs by the pool, ridding their bodies of pasty tan lines they'd picked up living in Southern California by baking topless underneath the blazing European sun. They'd douse themselves in fragrant oils of the slickest varieties and nuke their boobs until lunchtime. I'd usually join them to tan (with my top on), grimacing every time they flipped over and laid on their backs. Their nudity made me so uncomfortable, and it seemed such an unnecessary risk to take. What if someone saw them? Like Adem or a neighbor?

It was noon in the middle of the week—prime tanning hour at the house—when Colette dropped a magazine she'd been reading and sat up.

"We really need to get some pot," she said, breaking the silence. She saw that I was trying to avoid staring directly into her sunburned chest, and grabbed a shirt from the foot of her pool lounger. "Oh, sorry," she said, using one arm to hold a shirt over herself and the other to gesticulate her point. "Don't you think we need some?" she continued, using her pointer finger and thumb to demonstrate the act of smoking.

Even tanning, which was a peaceful activity I grew up enjoying, had become a mindless chore by this point. The monotony of doing nothing besides lying near a scuzzy pool for the entire three weeks we were in Toulouse, coupled with the awkwardness I felt in not being able to engage with my friend when she went topless, was becoming taxing. I needed a break from the house. A break from the boredom. And a break from the creepy animal parts inside of our basement bedroom that haunted me each night.

Even though Mom explained to me when I called her that the animal parts were being pickled—a culinary delicacy—I never felt at ease in the basement bedroom. I felt lonely and far from my home base, and I constantly second-guessed my decision to travel.

"That's a great idea," I said, standing up from my pool lounger. "It's so boring here, no offense."

We put a plan in motion and leaned on Celia to make it happen.

"There's a concert happening this weekend about an hour away," Celia told us when we confided in her. "I'll get us there."

Friday night came and the five of us packed into

Grandmother's car. We hopped in, buckled up, and rolled down all the windows. Celia hit the gas pedal and we were off. Our hair flew up to the ceiling, interlocking with one another's flyaways anytime she took a sharp turn around a bend.

We got to the concert quickly and parked inside a fenced-in field where there were lots of teenagers walking around aimlessly.

"This is gonna be hard. I mean, no one is just gonna walk up to us and sell us a bunch of drugs," Celia said, turning to us.

But then, as if the drug angels were listening to us talk, a barefoot guy in rolled up jeans walked by and said something to us.

"Guys, I swear that guy just said *foo-mare* or something. Doesn't that mean smoke? Go talk to him," Celia said, pushing Colette's shoulder.

Colette groaned, but then bounced over to him. He was taller than her, with a wiry beard that twisted down past his neck into a tangled mess.

Colette left his side and rejoined us. "He said he can sell us hash and he'll throw in a pipe," she said. "He asked who had the money and I pointed at you."

She was pointing at me.

I shushed her. "Keep your voice down. But what's hash?"

"I think it's like weed," she continued. "He says it comes in like a rock form or something. He tried to show it to me. It just looked like a stone. I'm not sure."

I opened up my triple-zippered wallet and dug around for money.

Mom had bought me a khaki nylon wallet to hide underneath my clothing for the trip. "No mugger could dare get through three zippers," she declared when we bought it from the travel store on Sepulveda Boulevard. Two zippers, maybe. Three? No way. She was probably right, too, because during the heat of the moment when I was trying to dig for money for hash, it took me quite some time to access my money. I found 800 Francs—the equivalent of around 150 American dollars—and handed it to Colette. It was nearly all the money I had to my name. The rest Mom was sending in biweekly payments to Adem for groceries.

"How much will this buy us?" I asked.

"I'll go find out." She went back to speak with the drug dealer and I asked Celia about hash, hoping she could tell me more. What if it was addictive and the gateway drug to more serious stuff, like what happened to Leonardo DiCaprio in the movie *Basketball Diaries* when he became addicted to drugs and lost everyone around him?

Colette returned minutes later, holding exactly what she described: a weird brown rock. The five of us snuck away to a row of portable toilets near a far end of the field, placed a small sliver of the brown rock inside the well of the pipe, and fired up a lighter.

Celia went first to demonstrate, then I followed, placing the wooden pipe to my mouth. It felt as though someone poured scalding hot soup down my throat and then asked me to gargle it around to achieve maximum discomfort.

"Whoa," I moaned.

Summer away from Mom was off to an amazing start.

⌇⌇⌇⌇⌇⌇⌇⌇⌇⌇

Mom sent me to France with a small notebook to keep a journal. It had an opalescent cover with a tiny seashell stitched into the center. On nights when I couldn't sleep—either because I got too high smoking hash or because I missed the overwhelming sense of comfort I found from being around Mom—I opened up my journal and started writing. Always poems, and never rhyming.

I liked to crawl into my own emotional cesspool, exploring what it meant to be alive, and what it meant to be alone. I wanted so badly to write about other things, like boys that I had crushes on back home, but when I flipped the shiny cover open and saw an empty page, I was compelled to dig. Poetry allowed me to access another layer of my consciousness.

While I never found the time to practice my oboe in France, I smoked and wrote nearly every day. Sometimes because I was bored, sometimes because I needed an escape, and sometimes because there was so much sibling rivalry and screaming in the house that I didn't know how else to cope.

The twins fought over everything, from boys to their father's new concubine, whom we nicknamed The Conk. I cringed whenever their shrill voices went above a certain octave.

Writing became my refuge.

It was the only place where they couldn't find me.

One particularly warm night, I was writing in my journal on the first floor when I spotted Celia's lanky legs walking down from her second story princess palace. She was waving her hands back and forth.

She belted to everyone in the living room: "I am going to kill Colette, where is that fucking slut sister of mine?"

I groaned and put my journal down.

Colette had been sneaking out of the house at night to make out with one of the French guys that Celia was dating, and since Colette always made a big fuss whenever she got ready to go out, asking us if her tops were tight enough and to pull the straps down on her bras, I assumed the whole house knew.

Weirdly, while having concubines and out-of-wedlock overweight kids was *tres* okay, evidently sharing French flings was not. The Conk was pissed to hear about Colette's disloyalty to her sister and took Celia's side, adding that Colette and Nicole were both whores (I know I was technically their friend, but they were). She yelled something in French then ran into the basement with Celia, in search of Colette. I went after them, and by the time I got down there, I couldn't believe what I saw.

Nicole was holding onto a chunk of The Conk's hair.

"We all hate you," Nicole shouted before pushing The Conk away.

I squinted to look at Nicole. There was something long and shiny in her hand. I looked closer. *Holy shit.*

Nicole cocked her wrist back over her shoulder and threw a knife at The Conk. It flew through the air like a boomerang and slammed against a wall.

Maybe it was a paring knife, or perhaps it was a nine-inch cook's go-to, but when that blade smacked the wall and bounced over to my foot, I saw myself dying. I saw the blade bouncing up from the carpet and catching enough speed that it went through my sock and pierced my leg, rendering me unable to walk. Then I saw no one caring and leaving me there to die in that dingy basement next to all those glass jars of pig feet and cow brains.

Next, shouting came from upstairs. It was Celia. She managed to sneak out of the basement while no one was paying attention and was back on the second floor, screaming.

We may as well have been in the movie *Clue*, where everyone darts around quickly and people run in groups from room to room, chasing loud screams and looking to solve a mystery. We hadn't quite gotten to the point where we discovered a dead body, but we had found the sister in the basement with a knife.

"You two are such fucking idiots. Don't ever talk to me

again," Celia shouted out of her window.

We peered out of the basement window and saw Celia manically throwing Colette's things out of her bedroom window. CDs fell quickly making loud splashes, while clothing delicately drifted down, settling on the top of the pool water like the first snow. I immediately wondered how Colette's things ended up on the top floor. *Had she been given permission to go up there without me?*

Adem moved to the foot of the staircase and turned to us. With a withering look on his face, he raised his hand and pointed a finger at me. "I am to call your mother."

I clutched my throat because for the first time in a long time, that's where my heart felt like it was lodged. I knew what was going to come next and I wasn't emotionally ready for it. As much as I longed to see Mom, part of me— perhaps the part of me that was discovering my independence or obsession with hash—did not.

Adem called Mom.

"She threw a knife, and now my concubine is scared for her life. The girls, they must leave now. I put them on a plane to the United States tomorrow."

"What? Adem, what are you saying?" Mom shouted on her end of the phone.

Mom was from Brooklyn, and it was only on the rarest of occasions that her calm tone changed course so drastically that someone could *hear* that she was, in fact, from

Brooklyn.

When Adem tried to intimidate Mom over the phone and said he was essentially kicking me out of his house and putting Colette and me on a nonstop flight to "anywhere in America," I knew instinctively that he was no longer speaking to kind, loving Samantha. He was on the phone with Margaret, and the person who should have been intimidated was not her, but him.

The second person who should have been intimidated and scared for their life was me. I was returning to the very place I'd spent the entire year trying to leave. And even though France was only a temporary escape, I'd failed. And somehow, Mom had won. She was right all along not to let me leave home.

In the morning, Adem came into the basement and woke Colette and me up early. "You're going to Newark, New Jersey," he commanded before adding that we had just 30 minutes to get our things and leave the house.

"Where is Newark?" I whispered to Colette, who was still in bed.

She rolled away from me. "Who fucking knows."

I flung my floral comforter back and raced out of bed and up to the first floor to call Mom. She answered on the first ring. "He's sending us to Newark, Mom," I told her. "Where is that?"

"It's okay. Your cousin will pick you up there and bring you to Grandpa's in Hampton Bays. I'll be there by the end of the week to meet you." The plan felt safe to me because we'd planned to meet Mom and Dad at Grandpa's anyway. Just not for another five weeks.

I hung up and darted downstairs, hastily stuffing everything I could identify as mine into my large duffel bag. In went a pile of dirty laundry and soggy wet bathing suits that had been drip-drying in the shower. Nicole and Mollie laid still on their mattress, avoiding us and awaiting their fate. They, too, were getting shipped off.

It wasn't until we landed in New Jersey and I saw my cousin April standing on the other side of customs that I realized I'd done something completely terrible. Up ahead, just a few yards in front of where my cousin stood waiting for me, government officials were going through luggage and inspecting travelers' personal belongings. I looked at Colette who was behind me in line and mouthed to her.

"Fuck."

She furrowed her brows and gave me a quick shrug of the shoulders.

I whispered to her. "The hash."

I faced forward in line to avoid looking suspicious then quickly looked back at Colette again, yanking on the straps of my duffel bag. "It's in my bag," I whispered again.

The rock of hash was the size of a nickel. Enough to notice if you wanted to find it. And what if they brought in a drug-sniffing dog? I was doomed.

I froze and held my breath. Before I could even think of a defense for myself, I was next. Any sudden darting out of line would have been a dead giveaway that I was guilty of something, so I just stood there completely blank-faced with my mouth agape.

I stared at the officer and handed him my passport and signed forms. I was so stupid. How could I possibly overlook something as monumental as packing drugs into my bag? This was taking my anti-mom revolt to a whole new level. I wanted to be so big and bad and poke holes in Mom's safety blanket, well this was certainly gonna do it. Pretty sure a 13-year-old smuggling drugs across the U.S. border would do the trick.

"Hello," I said sheepishly. I inhaled deeply through my nose and handed over my luggage to his colleague. My stomach grumbled, slowly beating up my insides. I clenched my butt cheeks and braced for the worst.

The officer looked closely at my eyes, then dipped his chin down to look at my passport. He looked at me again, then he looked at my passport, holding it open.

I was sweating from pores I never knew existed. My heartbeat was no longer a calm rhythmic song that signified life. It was a loud, jittery indication that I was going to get arrested. I was toast. I was sure of it.

He finally spoke. "Welcome back."

I ran to my cousin April and gave her a huge hug. "I need to use the bathroom, I'll be right back," I said.

I yanked my things into a stall and shut the metal door. I never had to poop so badly in my life. I plopped onto the toilet-seat cover and rested my elbows on my knees.

A summer away from Mom in France was supposed to deliver me with a thicker layer of courage. I was supposed to return to the United States a little less scared, and a little more in control. But now I'd been kicked out of France, and I nearly got caught for bringing drugs into the United States. The smartest thing would've been to flush the hash down the toilet. It's what Mom would've told me to do, but as I finished emptying my insides into the toilet and regaining consciousness, something clicked inside of me.

Even though I wasn't the reason we got kicked out of France, Mom had proved her point that it wasn't safe to leave Santa Monica. Someone had thrown a knife sort-of-at-me.

I didn't want Mom to be right. I took a deep breath and stood up from the toilet seat proudly, kicking the stall door wide open like a superhero.

I just smuggled drugs into America, I thought to myself. *Point, me.*

The Car Chase, 1997

Mom's cell phone was one of those massive Motorola flip phones that, if you put it in your purse or backpack, gave you a nagging neck ache by day's end. When I was 16 years old and started driving on my own, she never let me leave the house without it.

I was on my way to hang out with a boy named Leo when Mom came running after me down the walkway, a few feet behind. "Take the phone, honey," she shouted, holding the bulky device high into the sky like an Olympic torch. She caught me before I had a chance to get into the car and ignore her, so I took it and tossed it into my white pleather purse. Clunk. "Leave it on, but don't make any calls unless it's an emergency."

I raised my eyebrows high. "Ugh, I know."

"And make sure you lock your doors when you leave. I know how you like to drive into those neighborhoods."

"I knowwww," I roared back at her before slamming the car

door. She said "those neighborhoods" with what I thought was a gross affectation and it annoyed me, but she knew me well. I did like them. They were nothing like the perfect and boring area of Santa Monica where we lived and where I was too scared to do anything fun because Mom was always chasing me around with frightening statistics about gang violence, killer bees, and airborne pandemics, to name but a few.

I put her Isuzu Trooper into drive and headed south to hang out with Leo in Venice, certain sections of which I believed to be ruled by the Shoreline Crip gang because of newspaper clippings Mom would occasionally show me hoping to discourage me from ever spending time there. But I'd begun to enjoy the thrill of exploring new neighborhoods, especially places Mom had taught me were scary. If I successfully went and made it back in one piece, it would be a personal victory. According to Mom's data, 90 percent of the people that ventured into Shoreline Crip gang territory in Venice, California ended up with a knife wound, but I had an opportunity to become a proud member of the 10 percent.

Leo was a 10th grader at Venice High and we'd previously met at the Westside Pavilion mall. He was standing outside of Footlocker with a bunch of guys, and when I walked inside he stopped me and asked for my phone number. He said something compelling like, "Hey, let me get your phone number." Such a smooth line was hard to resist.

We started talking on the phone every few days or so, but the calls were always brief. He wanted to know what I was doing, what I was going to be doing, and if I wanted to come over tomorrow or the next day because his mom was going to be working the night shift at the hospital. I always said I was busy because I was nervous to go. I liked the idea of Leo, and I liked telling people at school about a boy that lived in Venice, but I wasn't ready to actually see him. Circling in the back of my head was the undeniable fact that if I accepted an invitation and went to his house, especially if his mom was gone, he'd want to make out. I'd made out with plenty of boys before and had lost my virginity a year prior to an ex-boyfriend, but I never looked forward to being intimate with anyone. Nothing particularly awful ever happened to me, but I always viewed hooking up as a high-pressure situation—one that caused me stress. I just liked talking.

What did appeal to me about the potential kissing, though, was the afterplay; the next day at school, when I could proudly brag about Leo to my classmates, the way a jock might boast about sleeping with a cheerleader. Dating someone that didn't go to Santa Monica High School earned you extra cool points, and I needed them. Desperate to create a "Leo story," I finally built up the courage to accept his invitation to hang out. It never occurred to me I could skip an actual hook up and just make up a Leo story.

I was in Mom's car and only a few blocks away from his house when a neon orange vintage Chevy Impala pulled up next to me at an intersection. I wasn't a car fanatic, but I knew how to spot low riders and other old school cars because they were so popular with the kids at my school. It didn't matter what academic class you were in, someone almost certainly had a picture of a custom painted Impala or Mustang slipped into the clear protective sheet on their three-ring binder. "I'm gonna get this car when I'm older," someone would say, pointing at the photo. Everyone would lean in and ogle.

In the driver's seat of the Chevy was a young guy maybe in his 20s. He had a flannel shirt on from what I could tell, and long brown hair that was slicked back. He swiveled his neck toward his passenger window and waved to get my attention. I glanced at him hoping he wasn't talking to me, but when we made eye contact I felt a rush of heat inside of my throat. Sheer terror.

The guy in the Impala shouted something out of his window, but I couldn't hear him over the sound of his blasting music. I assumed he was announcing, "You are dead meat," to me, or shouting out several sexual epithets. The threat was buried beneath the sound of my roaring heartbeat and his overpowering subwoofers. I needed to get away from this guy fast.

I never considered that he was trying to ask for directions or tell me that my tail light was out. No way. The guy was definitely going to drive me off the shoulder onto Rose Avenue, steal my purse which had Mom's phone in it, punch me in the face with the metal wrench you use to replace a flat tire because he obviously had one in his car, and leave me in a dumpster in an alley for the feral cats to come pick away at my skin. Fuck that.

I gripped my steering wheel tightly and turned the corner. Adrenaline surged through my upper body when I saw him turn the corner, too. I pressed my foot into the gas pedal, keeping one eye on the road and the other glued to my rearview mirror.

He was close on my tail and I could barely think. I spotted a gas station a few blocks up ahead and thought about pulling in, but I couldn't recall whether that was something Mom suggested doing or vehemently advised against.

As I approached the gas station I saw it was closed, so I pressed the accelerator even further into the floorboard and flew north on oddly empty Lincoln Boulevard back toward the safety of home. But the guy stayed on my bumper for three blocks, then four, occasionally slowing down to scream things out of his window at me and wave his metal tire wrench into the air like a gun. At a red light I made a last-minute sharp right turn on a small side street, turned up a dark alley, and shut off my headlights. The sound of my heart rate echoed in my ears. I cupped my right hand over my mouth to muffle my panting and bit my bottom lip.

A few seconds later he drove right past the alley. I held my breath and waited a few more minutes before putting the car back into drive and heading home with my lights still off.

Rather than pulling up in our driveway I parked the Isuzu halfway down the street, just in case the Impala owner caught up with me—he could have easily attached a magnetized GPS onto the car during the chase. Magnetized GPS trackers were about as difficult to install as a toaster. I reasoned that if I parked down the street then even if he found my car he wouldn't know which house was mine. Also, the sheer size of my house still embarrassed me, so just in case the guy wanted to be my friend and not rob me, he wouldn't judge me for having the biggest house on the block. I was covered on both ends.

I sprinted up the driveway, shoved my key in the lock, dashed in, slammed and dead bolted the front door, and set the alarm system. I'd narrowly escaped a knife shank from someone probably affiliated with the Shoreline Crips.

In the morning I poured myself a bowl of cereal and chewed quietly at the kitchen table. It was hard to eat. My teeth ached, and every bite made my stomach turn. I wanted to gag just thinking about what happened the night before. I was still so frightened; I almost died.

To calm down, I promised myself that I was never going

to speak to Leo again. Even if I enjoyed spending time in Venice, it just wasn't smart to go there. I also made a personal vow that I wouldn't meet any more boys from the Westside Pavilion. I'd keep things local and familiar.

I thought about telling Mom what happened but decided that it was best not to. I hated keeping secrets, they gave me so much uneasiness, but I just didn't want my parents to lay down the law and take their car away from me. As I washed my bowl over the sink Dad came into the kitchen carrying a large mangled orange traffic cone.

"Hey Beki, I found this impaled on the exhaust pipe."

"Oh shit," I said, immediately piecing together the previous night's activities. I must have driven over it before the guy tried to get my attention. "Sorry, Dad. I'll be more careful next time."

He walked out with the orange cone in his hand.

What the fuck was wrong with me? I had created the only plausible scenario for a story that started in "those neighborhoods."

At that moment my emotions went from being nervous to wanting to punch my fist through the window. Mom made me so scared to do anything she wasn't in favor of that I'd somehow convinced myself that I was incapable of doing them too. I had not just been in a car chase in Venice. Mom had chased me!

I clenched my jaw.

Smoking pot in random apartments or hanging out in Venice wasn't going to break me of my reliance on Mom; I had to do something major.

I redacted my decision to never venture to Venice and promised myself that as soon as I could become strong enough to leave home I would. Mom was the orchestrator of my fear and the only way to be truly tough would be to leave her.

Even if I had no idea how.

...and Other Things Mom Taught Me

Part II

Somewhere Over Colorado, 2000

"Are you alright?" a sweet, angelic flight attendant asked me about an hour into my flight.

There I was, soaring 30,000 feet above the United States—well above safety—and sandwiched in between Mom, who took the aisle, and Dad, who hoped that by pressing his forehead against the window he might have a shot at napping before we landed in Michigan on the red-eye from Los Angeles.

We were headed to the University of Michigan, where I was enrolled to start my freshman year of college. I'd been to the campus twice before, once to meet the volleyball coach and tour the campus—I'd been a competitive volleyball player since eighth grade and hoped to play for the Division 1 program—and another time to attend a pre-orientation with other incoming students from the West Coast, but this trip felt horribly wrong.

This trip was much more real and permanent.

"She's fine, just a nervous flyer," Mom answered to the

American Airlines angel. I gave Mom a blank stare and she squeezed the point of my elbow softly. I wanted to feel her hand on my skin—I desperately wanted to connect—but I was empty inside. The flight attendant nodded back at Mom as if she understood what was happening in our row and left us alone.

Dad pulled his head away from the greasy window and leaned in. "I'll never force you to do anything that makes you unhappy. Let's just get there and we'll talk." He shifted his weight back over to his right butt cheek and reassumed his position of discomfort against the cold glass. "Try and get some sleep," he mumbled. Then he nodded off.

I wasn't just a nervous flier, though. I was on my way to college. I was moving out of my parents' house, and the thought of it—the severity of leaving them—made me restless.

I was pretty sure my heart was not where it was supposed to be. It had vacated its normal location near my breastbone and was running around my body wildly, bouncing around the walls of my chest like a ball trapped inside of a pinball machine, pounding for me to hear. Or maybe it was I that was trapped. I pulled my elbow off the armrest and put my hands between my thighs.

"This is different," I said, rocking back and forth. "I can't breathe, Mom."

I really couldn't.

I thought back to the moment when I was accepted to the University of Michigan. I'd called Mom and Dad at Dad's office to share the news and could barely finish my sentence before Mom started screaming with joy. She was so proud of me. We both were. What happened to that girl? Why couldn't I access her on this plane?

When we landed in Detroit at 6:00 a.m. Central Time, I hadn't slept even one minute. Exhausted and drained from days of nonstop worry, I shuffled through the airport and toward Avis, where Dad rented an annoyingly shiny silver minivan. Earlier that summer Mom had taken me on coupon-crazy shopping sprees at Bed, Bath & Beyond in Los Angeles, where she bought me all the dorm necessities she decided I needed, including a large waste basket, shower caddy, and a printer. It all flew with us to Michigan. In the end I had nine pieces of luggage that we loaded into our minivan rental.

Dad pulled into a parking lot on campus in Ann Arbor. I hoped we wouldn't be able to find a spot and would have to circle for hours, but he found one within minutes. I peered out of the window and looked at my future. The University of Michigan was majestic, with buildings draped in storybook ivy and the ground covered in newly fallen leaves. I couldn't bare the sight of it.

"Do you want to change your clothes in the car first?" Mom asked. "You know, before you go inside and meet any-one?" She certainly wasn't one of those darling mothers that insisted her daughter wear pincurls in her hair and don red lipstick, but she did favor more formal clothing than the baggy sweatpants I had been wearing for 24 hours.

"No this is fine," I said, grumpily tugging at my University of Arizona hoodie, something I acquired during 11th grade when I dated a boy named James who attended U of A. I went to visit the campus, at least that's what my parents believed, but I also went to see him, which is how I bought the sweatshirt. I also went to a frat party and binged on Jungle Juice and vomited my brains out. It wasn't romantic, but I kept the sweatshirt as a reminder that I was once strong enough to leave home. Even if it was only to Arizona. For a day and a half.

I put on my best 'Happy Freshman At Check-In' face at U of M even though my outfit of choice looked like filthy gym clothes, made small talk with the annoyingly cheery volunteers in the lobby of my dorm, and hauled all nine of my duffel bags up to my room, with my parents following a safe distance behind. I waited for them before getting into the elevator, where they reminded me to be nice when I met my new roommate Erin.

"I willll," I whined, trying to sound as whiny as possible.

A slender girl in rolled up jean shorts and a navy blue Michigan sweatshirt greeted me at the door to my room. We exchanged a forced hug as I did my best not to squish her waify bones. She felt so frail. Erin and I spoke once on the phone when we found out we were destined to live together, but for some reason she looked different than I'd imagined. Smaller.

That summer when Erin and I spoke on the phone, she told me she was from Wisconsin and was "so excited" to be in an all-girls dorm with a "cool girl from California." She played the clarinet and was hoping to join the marching band when she got to campus, and she thought it was similar to how I hoped to walk onto the women's volleyball program.

"I flew out to meet the coach already, it was kind of a recruitment thing, they just didn't have any more scholarships left," I explained to her during the call, needing her to understand that playing an instrument was nothing like being a volleyball player, and the fact that I'd met the coach and sat in on a practice was really serious. I wasn't just joining a band. It annoyed me that she thought they were the same thing.

But now we were meeting in real life.

"I like your basketball shoes," she eagerly added after our hug, looking down at my red and white Michael Jordan sneakers. It was almost as if she gave me a quick sartorial evaluation from the top down, and finally got to the shoes and was like, "Okay, I guess I can compliment her on her shoes, because I'm pretty sure she's just wearing pajamas." It was a warm gesture on her part and given how tired I was I appreciated it.

"Want help unpacking your things?" she offered as I dragged in one duffel bag from the hallway. "I can help you when I'm done putting everything away." Her voice was high-pitched and filled with what I could only sense was joy. Immediately after my parents came in so did Erin's parents, who were brimming with happiness as palpable as their daughter's. Mom and Dad were glad to meet Erin's parents, but they were putting on the same fake smile I was. So after they exchanged hugs and hellos they politely excused themselves and said they were going outside to explore.

"That's a good idea," Erin's mom said. "Let's let the girls get acquainted." I gave Mom a half smile as she left our dorm room and opened my first bag. It was a long zippered duffel bag. I'd been dragging it across the floor for so long the edges had a small hole.

I hung up a few things in my tiny closet, then put all of the bags containing electronics in a sloppy pile.

"Well I'm all finished. I'm gonna meet my dad down on the grass right now so we can pick out a carpet," Erin said.

I hadn't even realized that our room was lined with linoleum. For whatever reason, it was up to the students to purchase their own wall-to-wall flooring which seemed like a complete waste of time and money.

"There's a bright purple one that's super," she cheerfully added on the way out the door.

I, an athlete, live in a room with a purple carpet? Yeah right. I chose not to insult her, though. "I'm gonna go eat with my parents, but yeah, purple is fine with me," I said apathetically.

I waited exactly 10 minutes after Erin left then darted out of the room, taking the emergency stairs down to the lobby, where I found my folks huddled near the vendors outside. Dad had his left hand on the small of Mom's back and they were slowly shuffling around the lush green quad. It was August and the Midwestern air was thick and heavy. It reminded me of the summers we spent at my Grandfather's house in Hampton Bays, New York.

All around us, bright-eyed students were purchasing bed trimmings to personalize their rooms. Mom was looking at a navy woven quilt with gold lettering on it when I ran up to them.

"She wants a purple carpet," I told them frantically while taking off my sweatshirt and wrapping it around my waist. "I can't do this."

Mom was having just as hard of a time with the move as I was, but for completely different reasons. "It's time for tough love," her friends suggested to her when she confided in them that she, too, was terrified for me to move thousands of miles away.

"What if she needs me and I can't get to her in time," she'd say back to them.

I'd applied to seven colleges. UCLA, UC Santa Barbara, UC San Diego, Tufts, George Washington, UNC Chapel Hill, and University of Michigan. The UC schools felt like the obvious thing to pursue—everyone was doing it—but when I received my UCLA rejection letter, I lost interest in the other two California campuses. Santa Barbara and San Diego had less than impressive athletic programs, and that was always the biggest selling factor for me. I was a good volleyball player—not fantastic—but I was devoted to the sport and needed to attend a school with a dominant Division 1 athletic program. I wanted Dad to turn on the television and see my school's college basketball team playing and call me. That wasn't going to happen if I went to UC San Diego.

I also applied to college as my idealized self. I believed that I could go to any state I wanted and succeed, because that's who I wanted to be. And my parents loved that idea. They loved thinking that, despite how weak and scared I'd been as a child, that I'd somehow pulled it together enough to manage living far away. Living close to home wasn't a priority for my idealized self.

I looked at Mom on the Michigan quad wanting to see "old Mom." The one who would pull me in close and rescue me. She slipped the quilt back onto the vendor's pile and made eye contact with Dad. I could tell she needed him to do the talking.

"I don't know what else to say," Dad said, having an easier time delivering the necessary "tough love" lines. "All we want you to do is give it a chance. Just six, no, try one month. Just try one month for us and see how it feels. You can always come back home, but you can't always have this."

Everything he said was reasonable.

I had been transparent about my desire to get away from home and Los Angeles. I could have applied to any school I wanted—I *did* apply to any school I wanted, and I chose Michigan. My parents pushed, sure, but I chose it. Yet there I was standing in the center of it all and I wanted out. I wanted to snap my fingers and be instantly transported back to Santa Monica, where I felt safe and in control. A month sounded like an eternity. I knew I wouldn't succeed. There was nothing they could say that would make me feel comfortable staying even one night.

"I can't do it. I don't even want to sleep here. Can I sleep in your hotel room tonight?" My legs jittered. A corset was cinched around my chest. The world was closing in on me. I felt like I was losing them. Like I was being orphaned in a stupid state in a stupid part of the country, and I'd put myself there.

Dad saw my hands shaking. "You're breaking my heart," he said softly.

My eyes burned with sadness and I began to tremble hysterically. "Can we please go stand somewhere else?"

"We love you and we hate seeing you this way," he added.

Then I broke Dad. His eyes filled with tears.

The jittering became more intense. I needed to run, and fast. I needed superhero capabilities that would allow me to sprint directly out of campus, out of Michigan, and be back in California before night.

"Please, can we leave?" I pleaded.

We left my things in my room and went to eat lunch in town.

Finally, I could breathe for a second.

The restaurant was busy. Gleeful students and their ever proud parents spilled out onto the street, while their younger siblings looked up at them in admiration. They smiled and laughed and made references to the campus and dorms. I wanted to plug my ears and push my way through to get inside the restaurant, like a running back sneaking through the defense.

Inside, maize and blue pendants covered every inch of the restaurant's interior. Even Mom and Dad were wearing Michigan crewneck sweatshirts. And there I was, in head-to-toe gray toting a school sweatshirt that said Arizona.

I was being swallowed whole.

We chewed our lunch quietly, perhaps hoping that the person who broke the silence would eventually give in and agree to the other's demands. I closed my eyes, knowing I was going to lose this one. "Please just let me go home," I said meekly.

Before I could finish Mom tossed her napkin onto the table.

"I can't listen to this anymore. Do whatever you want."

Then she crossed her arms in her lap and started crying.

Biting nausea coursed through my body, through my limbs and around my head, landing in the back of my throat like a bomb ready to detonate.

I'd had this feeling before.

This paralyzing fear so perverse that dry heaving would have been a relief in comparison. I wasn't choosing to leave campus; my body was physically rejecting it. I had no option but to listen to my insides, why couldn't they see that? If I were suffering from a generic headache, I'd have to listen to the headache; respond to it. Maybe Tylenol, or maybe water would do it. There, in that restaurant, my *body* was suffering and needed me to respond to it.

It needed to be removed from the state of Michigan immediately.

"Why are you being so mean?" I whined, crying again. "It's not that I don't want to stay here, I *can't* stay here," I finished. Other diners looked on, curious as to why I was crying, but I didn't care.

"Beki, you'll have to do this alone," Mom said, waving to get the attention of the waitress. "I can't watch you do this to yourself, it's killing me." She dropped her head slowly and cupped her hands around her face.

I wanted them to tell me it was okay. That they forgave me and that they understood. But they wouldn't give me that satisfaction, and their disappointment made it that much harder;

it made the nausea that much more virulent. There was no one on my side to help me, and I hated Mom for abandoning me there. She was the one that made me fear the world, and now there I was, an enrolled student at the fucking University of Michigan, completely paralyzed by those fears. There wasn't a single strand of DNA in my body that knew how to be that student. I only knew how to run away.

So on my first day of being in college while my peers were busy personalizing their bunk beds, buying purple carpets, and playing ice breakers to determine who, if anyone, was still a virgin, I made my personal stamp on freshman experiences by doing the ultimate walk of shame. I headed back to my dorm, handed over my Wolverines ID card to the volunteers in the lobby, re-rented a luggage cart, and dragged all of my bags back into the elevator. Erin wasn't in the room at the time, but a few girls I'd met down the hall saw me and asked me what I was doing. I kept my eyes glued to the ground and ignored them. I didn't even leave Erin a note; I just emptied my side of the room and vanished. The "cool girl from California" wasn't that cool after all.

I slept the entire flight back home.

Once in L.A. I lied to everyone about the number of nights I slept in my dorm room (it varied from two nights to a week), and more importantly, my reason for leaving college. Sometimes I made Erin into a *Single White Female* roommate from hell that was trying to steal my identity. Curious friends would want the details. "How, exactly, was she a crazy roommate like Jennifer Jason Leigh in *Single White Female?*" they'd ask. I'd fumble around for a reason, trying to parse together scenes from the film, but it had been so long since I'd actually seen it that I'd end up just saying things like, "It's hard to explain."

But even when I tried to tell the truth, I couldn't come up with anything good. The truth was that I didn't have a good reason. I panicked the same way I did when I tried to walk to school with Lo and the time I tried to drive to Venice, except this time, the consequences of this fear-driven decision were monumental. I left college before it even started and there was no going back. Everyone was disappointed in me, from my brothers to my friends. There wasn't a single loving hand that caressed my cheek and said, "It's okay, you did the best you could."

I desperately wanted that.

Everyone assumed I bailed on Michigan because I was homesick and too attached to Mom, and as weeks passed and the anxiousness of what I had done faded, I couldn't help but allow my confusion to turn into anger. I was so mad at myself for giving up. Homesickness was something that happened to weak children, it wasn't something that was supposed to happen to a college-bound 18-year-old athlete.

I spent days hiding in my room, evaluating my behavior.

How could I want something so badly, be given it, and then willingly sabotage it all? And more importantly, why hadn't Mom prepped me for this type of mental attack during all our years of survival schooling? I knew how to fight off robbers near Macy's, why didn't I know how to fight for myself?

Or, really, how to fight myself.

~~~~~~~~~

The first emotion my parents felt was anger, and the only way they knew how to process that sensation was to give me the silent treatment. But then the guilt quickly followed. They hung their faces in shame, like they'd set me up for failure, and they were determined to help me get back on track.

It was early September by the time my parents spoke to me again and they reminded me that I had one shot at attending a University and redeeming myself: UC Santa Barbara, a school I hated when I first went to visit because I hated everything. My older brother Damon had graduated from UCSB 12 years prior, so he volunteered to take me on a tour when I was still in high school and evaluating my college options. Before I even decided on the University of Michigan.

Since 10th grade I'd come to the conclusion that anyone who drank beer or smoked pot was supremely stupid—I did it throughout the seventh grade and stopped the year after, so the people that still indulged in drugs were pathetic.

When people suggested I even consider a party school like UCSB, I rolled my eyes. Plus, the Santa Barbara volleyball program was considered the cream of the crop: Division I Top 10, which meant that I'd never have a shot of making the team. When Damon took me on the tour months back, I counted the number of students I saw drinking beers out on their front patios and did all the math I needed to.

The place was a zero.

But UCSB didn't look all that bad when September 1st, 2000 hit and I didn't have a college to attend. Santa Barbara was on the quarter system and wouldn't start for another three weeks, and since they accepted me previously, all I needed to do was find a way to get back in. It was my only option.

I sent compelling letters to the school dean and put myself on every waitlist I could. A week before the fall quarter began I received a phone call from the Admissions Department. They said I could enroll, but they couldn't guarantee that I'd be able to get into the classes I wanted or find on-campus housing. Thinking about commuting 100 miles each way from my parents' house was dreadful, but I was thankful to get in. Mom, who'd been struggling with her own internal battle of how to help me without coddling me, eventually came to my rescue and sent the Director of Housing a bouquet of flowers, which I guess worked, because after just two weeks of commuting or squatting at my friend Summer's apartment on Del Playa Drive, I received a housing assignment: an eight-person suite on the edge of campus in San Rafael Residence Hall, an international and upperclassmen transfer dorm. My suite-mates included two bulimics and one girl who used wash-cloths in lieu of sanitary napkins when she menstruated. We were a mixed bag of students with odd college paths.

The suite had four bedrooms, a bathroom with two showers, and a shared living room with couches and a TV. I moved into a bedroom with a junior transfer student named Molina Modina who liked to say her full name as much as possible because it rhymed and she thought people enjoyed that.

Molina Modina had the room to herself for a full two weeks before I arrived, so she was surprised and even con-fused when I showed up and asked her if I could have one of the twin beds. Assuming she had hit the jackpot and not been assigned a roommate, she arranged the beds next to each other to form a queen bed directly in the center of the room. When she obliged and gave me one of her beds, she didn't bother to scoot hers to a corner, so for the duration of our time together, Molina Modina's pink satin bed was centered perfectly in the room, and I crammed everything I could into a corner against the window curtains.

When my friend Summer came to visit and see how I was doing in my new place, she was visibly perplexed to see our layout. "Why are the beds set up like this?" she asked. Having been a freshman just a year prior herself, she knew that there were only so many ways to set up the rooms.

But Molina Modina didn't share the same vision when it came to decor. "What do you mean?" she asked, adding an uncomfortable giggle and uptick at the end of her sentence.

Even though I had my own address and was technically in college, I wasn't ready to spend weekends in Santa Barbara, so I enrolled in three Tuesday-Thursday courses. I was so committed to taking Tuesday-Thursday classes that I even fudged some admissions paperwork so that I could sign up for a pre-calculus class that I wasn't academically qualified to take. I lied and told the admissions office I'd already taken pre-calculus in high school, which I, of course, hadn't. Every Thursday when I finished class, I got into my car and drove the 100 miles to Los Angeles. It was the only thing that felt right. Sometimes traffic was so bad that it took me three hours to get home, instead of the usual one and a half. Still, there was no way I was spending a weekend on campus. I was too nervous.

Because I was wasting so much time in transit, I turned the back of my inherited Isuzu into a closet of sorts, squeezing a three-drawer cabinet into the trunk; that way I always had enough clothes on me when I went home. When my parents started to express worry over seeing me in their house every weekend instead of on campus, I'd sleep at a friends house in Santa Monica instead. I needed to be at least near them in order to feel safe.

My current radius of independence maxed out at 100

miles, and I was perfectly fine with that. One hundred miles away, four days a week, felt like a huge leap forward in my chaotic search for independence.

Tropicana Garden Apartments, 4:30 a.m

The bright red light from the bedroom alarm clock in Apartment 315 at the Tropicana Garden Apartments was the only thing I could see through the horizontal cracks between my eyelids and my eyes. It was practically laughing at me.

Ha, you're awake again!

It was one of those crappy alarm clocks from the drugstore that was supposed to have a buzzer and radio option, but you could never really get a station to come in reliably, so it pretty much only beeped when you set it. That morning the 4:30 a.m. screen beamed into my face the way an angry cop might hold a flashlight at the window of an irresponsible driver.

I must have been the only person awake in all of Santa Barbara and the alarm clock wanted me to know it.

Smashed next to me on a small twin bed was my boyfriend Charles. He was five feet ten inches tall—the first guy I dated that was taller than me—and skinny, with thighs smaller than mine. We met on the UCSB campus at a dance, which sounds nerdy to have attended a college dance, but it was held by the campus multicultural society and we met while grinding to the R&B song "Peaches & Cream" by 112. Not so nerdy. When the song ended he politely asked me if I wanted to sit down and talk, so we moved to the side of the room and sat on an empty buffet table, where I quizzed him on his extracurriculars. Dancing to good music wasn't enough to keep my interest; I needed to know how he felt about Santa Barbara...specifically if he drank and smoked. I needed to know if he disliked Santa Barbara as much as I did.

A shared hatred of beach bums on bikes was something I longed to find in a romantic partner.

It was a relief to learn that he didn't drink, smoke, or care for bums. He did, however, kind of like Santa Barbara. Even with his poor choice in schools, Charles couldn't have been more ideal so we started dating. First hanging out on campus after class, then going out to dinners at Chili's Grill & Bar and eventually, at 4:30 a.m. on that awful night, sleepovers.

Together we weighed 300 pounds and had over 11 feet of knobby limbs, none of which had any space in his small wooden bed. After a night of fine Tex-Mex fare and a makeout session on his couch, we got into his bed at 1:30 a.m. His roommate was out elsewhere so we had the place to ourselves. Charles fell asleep almost as soon as his skin hit the pillow, and I tried my hardest to follow him. It was our first time spending the night together—my first time ever sleeping next to a guy—and with every minute that passed I became increasingly more aware of the fact that I wasn't sleeping. I stared aimlessly at Charles and thought my not sleeping was an indication that something was wrong; my body was alerting me. Maybe it was wrong of me to be there. *It's too soon for us to have a sleepover*, I decided. I needed a minute to myself—some space to figure out what was happening to me, so I pushed my palm up against his muscular shoulder and shook him. His skin was soft and almost tender, but I was ice cold and needed him to be far away from me.

"Charles, take your roommate's bed," I said in a heavy whisper. Without even responding, he rolled out of bed, put one foot on the ground and used the other to propel himself into his roommate's empty bed, where he resumed his perfect sleep cycle almost instantly. It was an athletic move and I watched him in bewilderment.

The fucker is doing toe twirls and still sleeping, I thought. I looked at the clock. 4:40 a.m. I told myself that the time didn't matter, I would be okay even with just a few hours of shut eye. But even alone in his bed with his heavy blanket all to myself my mind whipped and whirled in circles. Up and down, left and right. *Maybe I'm not sick, maybe I'm dying*, I wondered. My heart beat fast and I put two fingers against my carotid artery to feel it pulsing.

Dup-dup. Dup-dup.

It got faster, sometimes barely squeaking out the du before hitting the next Du-du-du-du. I needed to get out of his apartment. I took one enormous inhale through my nose, sat up, and leapt out his bed. Lightning speed was on my side, enabling me to get dressed in what felt like five seconds.

I left immediately.

I arrived at the San Rafael Residence Hall within 10 minutes, but I sat in bed shivering and waited until 6:30 a.m. to call Mom. Climbing into my own sheets wasn't as soothing as I'd hoped it would be, and I knew what was missing was Mom's familiar voice. I wanted to hear her tell me that I was okay. That I wasn't dying.

She answered immediately and asked if I was in danger. It was the third quarter of school and I hadn't been home to visit since I met Charles a month prior.

I poured my heart into the phone when I heard her voice, practically hyperventilating every time I tried to speak. I knew she would be upset if I told her I was out sleeping at a guy's house—she was always so quick to worry that I'd all of a sudden become a slut—so I lied and explained that I was too scared to sleep in my own bed, and that I was having trouble just breathing.

"I'm so scared," I told her, sobbing. I coughed and whined and jerked my body around the bed. "Maybe I should get in the car and drive home," I said, my throat closing up as soon as I said it.

Molina Modina dropped out of school at the end of the first quarter and went back to community college in her hometown, so I had our room all to myself. Mom sat quietly and listened to me cry.

"Don't do that, honey," she said, causing me to shake even more. It was the exact opposite of what I wanted her to say, and she could hear it in my erratic breathing, so she conceded to ease my pain. "Come later in the morning. I'll make you breakfast. Just rest a few hours before you get in the car, okay?"

"Okay, so I can come home?" I said, double-checking.

"Yes, Rookie. Just take a short nap before your drive," she said, cradling her voice around me. By then my tears had dried on my cheeks in a mound of what felt like hardened snot, and it seemed as though no more were coming.

At 11:07 a.m. I woke up with the phone nestled in my chest and called Charles to apologize. He was surprisingly forgiving and asked if I wanted to hang out later. I then called Mom and told her I wouldn't be coming home after all.

"I always want to see your face but I'm happy to hear that," she said. "Do you want to talk about what was really going on?" she then asked, insinuating that there was more to the story than I'd let on. It pissed me off how quickly she was able to go from soothing mother to private investigator.

"Actually, I have to go. The cafeteria is going to close for breakfast soon."

They'd already stopped serving breakfast.

Although I snuck out on Charles on our first night alone, we continued to see each other. We met on campus for lunch, found each other at parties, and even went out on dinner dates to various chain restaurants in Santa Barbara, ordering adult dishes I'd never tried before, like spinach and artichoke dip and pita chips with fancy hummus.

"I need you to leave! Are you up?" I said late on our second attempted sleepover night, nudging him awake from another seemingly perfect slumber. I was a trooper, so I tried to calm myself by breathing slowly before I had to put an end to my own personal misery and get rid of the happily snoring loaf next to me. In through the nose, out through the mouth.

It was no use.

Everything with Charles was wonderful when the sun was up, but much like a vampire or even Cinderella, life changed for me when the clock struck 12. I dreaded nighttime with Charles, and having him lie next to me was insufferable. It had nothing to do with being anxious about sex— we'd already done it—it was just about his presence. Sleep, as it seemed, became something I was no longer capable of achieving as long as he was in the room.

He jerked his head off the pillow and looked up startled. "What? What's wrong?"

"I need you to go home, right now. Please, Charles. Get

up." My arms shook underneath the sheets.

"Again?" He rubbed his eyes and reluctantly looked at his watch. "But, it's 4:15 in the morning. You want me to walk home right now?" He laid back down, hoping that I'd forget I just asked him to leave my dorm.

"Yes, I'm sorry." I continued. I then tried to describe the crippling rage happening inside of my body to him, but he had fallen back asleep. I believed with all of my might that the terrible feeling would go away once he left—it had to—so I stopped talking and finished by insisting he leave.

With his eyes shut he asked if I was mad at him. Kind of? Not mad at him, *per se*, but at what he represented: someone that could doze off. "Why don't I just go lie on the couch?" he asked. Since I was living in a suite, there were couches in the living room that he could have easily gone to sleep on, and a wooden door to separate us, but that wasn't far enough. My body wasn't in the mood to compromise.

This time I was firm. "No, I need you to go home."

And because Charles was superiorly nice, he left. Every other weekend we'd try our luck at another overnight, and each time we failed. He sucked it up for weeks, hanging his head in a hazy daze while stammering home in the early morning Santa Barbara fog. I'd always call to apologize, usually around mid-day because falling asleep after 4:00 a.m. warrants a late wake-up call.

Charles liked me, or rather "day me," so he dealt with it as best he could for as long as he could. But when our fresh-man year was coming to a close and we still failed to have a pleasant slumber party, he grew impatient.

"Have you ever thought about going to see a therapist to talk about your sleeping problems?" he asked one day during our Psychology 101 lecture. I loved that we had class together—finding a seat next to him in our huge 700-person class always made me feel so mature. "You know, it could help," he said, moving around in his seat to get comfortable.

Even though I knew Charles had been physically pres-ent each time I manically kicked him out of bed for reasons that were unknown, I naïvely hoped he hadn't noticed that it happened, or that it wasn't that big of a deal. I wanted him to view my inability to sleep next to him in the same way he would if he were dating a girl that had a food allergy. *No peanuts for me!* So when he suggested I see a therapist I was downright appalled.

"Is it really that big of an annoyance?" I whispered to him in lecture.

A loud burst of air shot out of his nose. Then he shrugged his shoulders ever so slightly. I knew from his ges-ture and dramatic exhale that the answer was yes.

It really was that big of an annoyance.

Being mentally unable to relax next to someone I wanted to be with was above and beyond anything my freshman psych class could help me make sense of. I spoke with my parents about it—honestly this time—and they agreed that I should see someone.

"Don't forget all the trouble you had sleeping as a kid," Mom reminded me before adding, "I'm going to ignore the part about you sleeping at a guy's house for now because I want you to be happy and figure out what's going on." Mom always tried to lighten the mood with humor.

That week I went to see the school psychologist.

Our meeting was brief, more like an evaluation than a conversation, but I told the psychologist what was happening to me at night. He took some notes in a small book, then said I should pick up a referral at reception. He suggested I see Dr. Schwinn at the Anxiety and Panic Disorder Clinic of Santa Barbara. I left the health center feeling both proud and embarrassed. Proud that there was something wrong with me that I could go back and use to justify my behavior to my parents and Charles, and embarrassed that there *was* something wrong with me.

And what was an Anxiety Clinic anyway? What was anxiety?

Two weeks later I got in my car and drove to the clinic. While the building lacked any character and blended in with all the other brown Spanish-style structures around it, the words "Anxiety and Panic" were written enormously on the front. They seemed as large as the famous Hollywood sign. I parked at a meter and quickly went inside, hoping no one would see me. Whatever anxiety was, I didn't need people to know I had it.

Dr. Schwinn was waiting for me in his office when I arrived. He stood up from his chair when I opened the door, just enough to reach out his arm and shake my hand. The sleeve of his brown sports coat slid ever so slightly, revealing strands of gray hair on his wrist.

I took a seat on the far end of a mustard-and-cocoa plaid couch and scooted to the center, where the two cushions met. He smiled at me politely, waiting for me to finish fidgeting. There was a small woven pillow on the edge of the couch. I picked it up and put it on my lap.

"So tell me about why you're here," he began.

I looked across the room at his bookcase and wall decor. Everything in his office was mostly brown and bland, just like the exterior of the building, and a green banker's light sat on his desk, illuminating the texture on his jacket. I could see now that it was corduroy.

"I can't sleep, I'm up all night sweating," I blurted, twirling the pillow in my hand. I continued, "I freak out at night and end up hysterically shaking in bed. I get so cold and I shake obsessively."

He nodded slowly, staring at me through his perfectly circular glasses. "Is there anything in particular that you think about at night?"

"Death. Aloneness. Being Dead." I jumped when I said

it. It was the first time I'd articulated it.

"That's interesting," he told me. "Is anyone around you sick?"

I shook my head no.

"Anyone close to you recently die?"

I shook my head no.

He continued. "Alright, can you tell me more about your fear of dying then?"

I rested the pillow again in my lap. "I don't know. I get scared a lot at night, always and only at night. If I sleep with my boyfriend his presence will make me sick and I'll need him to leave, but it will also just happen when I'm alone. I'm terrified of being dead and I obsess over it at night. The only thing that calms me down is when I call my mom."

"So you're worried that you're going to die in your sleep?"

"No," I said, raising my voice. He didn't get it at all. "I'm not scared I'm going to die, I'm scared of being dead." I readjusted myself on the couch. "I," I paused. "I don't want to be dead."

My neck was tight. It was at that moment that I became aware of the fact that I wasn't a prototypical patient concerned about the various ways in which I could be struck by a speeding car or robbed at gunpoint (I was a student in Santa Barbara; the only dangerous people there were hungry vegans on beach cruisers—except for the month before when a freshman screaming "I am the angel of death" drove his 1991

Saab into five students, killing four), I was actually terrified about the inevitability of death. That no matter how much I'd been taught to *be* safe and how to avoid dangerous situations, there was nothing I could do to avoid death.

I hated thinking about what was going to happen to me once I became dead, assuming that whatever it is, I'd have to live with that forever.

Like a bad tramp stamp.

Our first session ended and I went outside and into my car to call my parents.

Dad answered. "I need to come home," I said, before telling him anything about the session.

"We are so proud of you," he started. Mom talked over him in the background. Her voice carried louder than his.

I yelled into the phone. "I can't hear you over Mom."

"Sam, would you stop that?" he shouted. "Beki, I'm putting you on speaker."

I told them I wanted to go home. They told me they were proud of me for seeking help and that I needed to stay put. Mom said she'd come up to visit me soon. "You're the toughest girl I know," she yelled.

Despite feeling that Dr. Schwinn didn't understand my perspective or my fear, he diagnosed me with something called a panic disorder and suggested that I pursue cognitive treatment with him. I'd never even heard of a panic disorder before, but I accepted his evaluation as fact and agreed to the treatment anyway. I was alone in a strange city experiencing strange sensations at night that were only getting increasingly worse. So much so that by the time I first visited him, I'd begun to fear nighttime completely. The awareness of the looming moon would unhinge me, forcing me to fixate on only the maudlin: being dead, or worse, my parents being dead. Living 100 miles away from them was a fact I could stomach during the day; at night, however, all it did was create a heightened awareness of being alone.

And alone was something I'd always dreaded.

I was desperate. If Dr. Schwinn had told me an entirely different reason I was feeling this way I would have given him the same nod and signed up for the same number of follow-up sessions. I felt like flotsam in an unfamiliar, menacing ocean, and as much as I knew he was a stranger that barely knew me, he was the only person that had the potential to throw me a lifejacket.

Even if it didn't quite fit correctly.

Two days later I went back for our second session and he gave me a "brain assignment" so that I could get back into the driver's seat, so to speak.

"I'd like you to sit on your bed during the day or during a time in which you feel safe and scribble everything that terrifies you about being dead," he said. "Here, write it in here." He handed me a brand new legal pad. "Everything that scares you about death, make sure you write it down. Once you have it all, I'd like you to read it back to yourself every single afternoon."

"That sounds awful," I shouted. Just the thought of doing something so twisted made me uncomfortable. "I don't want to do that at all."

"It's an exercise and I'd like you to try," he said plainly. "Do what you can and let me know how it goes."

I left his office and went home. I sat on my bed, locked the bedroom door, and began to write, starting with the most obvious.

Being dead is forever. It never ends.

Never, ever, ever.

I'll never see my family again.

I'll be alone.

No one will come get me.

Whoa. The back of my throat started to burn and close up. I'd only written five lines down and I was already tormented inside. I had no idea where these visceral feelings were coming from—no one was sick, no one immediate had died. It was completely irrational, yet all-consuming. I put the notepad down and went to the bathroom to wash my face, returning later to finish writing. I pushed the pen hard into the pad, closed my eyes, and let it all pour out, writing faster and faster with each added thought.

When I came up for air I had two pages worth of notes. They were surreal; all about death and aloneness. It felt so unfair that I'd only get to be a participant in life for such a small interval of time. It was unfair and temporary, and if it was all going to be ripped away from me what was the point of trying to achieve anything in life; what was the point of trying to connect with anyone?

I didn't need to find the meaning of life, I needed to find the permanency in it.

I cringed when I looked at my notes. Who would write such dark and demented stuff? This wasn't my handwriting; it had to be a journal from David Lynch. I would never write these things. Not "day me," at least. Each sentence teetered between brutally pithy and deeply existential, as if I believed if I wrote a sentence enough times I could think of a way around death and perhaps even outsmart it before the sentence had to end.

Before my life had to end.

I glanced at the words in complete horror and hid the notebook under my pillow, embarrassed at what I'd even written down. There wasn't a person in my life, not Mom, not Dad, and not Charles, that knew these thoughts were swirling in my head, but they were there, consuming all my quiet moments. I rarely acknowledged they were up there, but as I sat in my bed I saw them, staring back at me from a lemon yellow notepad, written with an ugly gray ink pen that I'd thought was black when I bought it from the school bookstore.

The next afternoon, I sat in bed and read my obsessively dark memo back to myself. Then I did it the next day. And the day after that. Sometimes I'd cry and wail and throw the notepad against the wall and pound my fists into my bed until I was too exhausted to cry any more, other times I'd end up with my knees pressed against the bathroom floor and my head hovering over the toilet bowl fearful that I'd have to throw up. I usually didn't. Sometimes when the homework got too intense or the afternoon crying left my throat burning from all the heaving, I'd call Mom just to hear her voice. I'd tell her that I didn't have such a hard time sleeping when I lived at home. This would all go away if I transferred schools. Maybe city college would be better for me the way it ended up being better for Molina Modina, I'd add. Although, I had no idea what the hell happened to Molina Modina.

I was infuriated when Mom told me not to make any decisions without speaking to Dr. Schwinn.

Every week or so I went back to see him to talk about my homework. I'd tell him how much I hated it, and about the abdominal stress. The anxiety made me empty out my insides until there was nothing left of me.

"You are undergoing exposure therapy, and this is all normal," he explained.

Normal.

I liked being told I was normal.

When I wasn't being confronted with my own fears, Dr. Schwinn would ask me about my relationship with my parents, especially Mom, and I'd cry on command. He could say something as innocuous as "What's your mom's favorite food?" and I'd lose it. My mind would fast-forward through every positive thought and immediately land on the worst one: the inevitable last day with her when I'd be left to drag my feet on this planet without her. A simple mention of Mom would make my scalp sweat because I knew I wouldn't have her forever.

The day he asked me if I ever thought about my mom dying sent me down an emotional drain. My head spun, and I spent the entire next day locked in my room hiding beneath my comforter. I never wanted to talk about that with him again.

It was then that it became clear that my fear of death was directly connected to my obsession with and dependency on Mom. For the first time in my life I saw her as an ally and less as a parent, and I was terrified to ever lose her. I'd spent so much of high school in angst, mad at her. Mad at her for raising me to be such a scaredy-cat; mad at her for never letting me do anything I wanted; mad at her for making us live in a big house that resulted in everyone acting intolerably toward me in high school. I finally was getting to know Mom. And getting to know me.

I was 18 years old, and, while still immature, it was as though I'd just met her for the first time in my life. I stopped being annoyed with her and replaced the contempt with what felt like boundless love. Love so immense that I'd only get to enjoy it for a few precious moments before the "What if Mom dies one day" sadness would eat me up, choking my throat and gripping the edges of my heart, sending it, and then me, flying toward an intangible evil. The feelings I had toward my mother were a dangerous cocktail, mixed with addiction and intense love.

Throughout treatment I felt increasingly sadder and more alone. While I was armed with information that I'd never had before, I was still panicking. I never felt any better. I never slept any better. The only real calmness I felt existed in the small period of time after an attack finished. Much like the way someone with the stomach flu would feel better immediately after throwing up. The post-vomit, or post-panic, was a farce, but it always felt so good.

Like I could float in that short moment forever.

I'd learned my panic disorder was genetic on some level and I made the mistake of telling Mom that. I'd never seen her have an anxiety attack before, but I did know her to always be in some sort of war-like preparation for battle… for an actual attack. So one day after another frustrating session with Dr. Schwinn, I called Mom to ask her if she had panic attacks.

"Mom, do you think, maybe, you have this too? I mean, you're scared of a lot of stuff, right?" I asked. I wanted to be useful, but I sounded inarticulate.

Mom didn't answer. Instead, she cried.

"Mom?" I asked quietly into the phone.

"I'm so sorry I did this to you," she said. "I had no idea what I was doing. The only thing I wanted to do was protect you, and instead, my own fears ended up giving you panic attacks."

"You're being so hard on yourself. Did you ever think it was Grandpa that made you this way? He made you scared of everything."

We were both silent after that. Mom was a tough, key ring-toting, ready-to-fight-a-thief woman, but I'd just shot her with something she couldn't process.

Then she started listing all the times in my life in which I missed out on something because of fear. She fired them off at me as if she had them written down at her bedside. "Look what happened to you at Michigan, my God, I made you fearful and you ended up missing out on something you worked hard for and deserved."

"Mom, it's okay," I told her, mostly lying. Knowing that the anxious feelings I developed over my lifetime had something to do with the way she raised me—and the way she was raised—was confusing, and recognizing my completely debilitating reliance on her was scary. I wanted Mom to be in control like she'd always been, because it made my role in life easy: the angry kid who got to blame her parents for various injustices.

"This is why you left Michigan, I'm so sorry I did this," she went on. But while that was intended to be a continuation of her already long apology, it triggered something in me that I hadn't dealt with. Latent rage about what I'd done.

I never allowed myself to fully process that period of time; I'd never accepted responsibility for my behavior, even partial. I abandoned Michigan.

Me.

I screamed at Mom over the phone. "Why are you bringing Michigan up?" Then I pressed the off button on my cell phone with all my might and slammed the phone down into my bed, hoping that the noise would reverb into her handset at home.

Four hours passed before guilt set in and I called back.

When she said hello she sounded somber and flat, as if I'd done something hurtful to her. I was unstable on the phone, demanding she—overprotective, insanely prepared, and kooky Mom—come back to me.

"Mom, it's okay, seriously," I insisted. "Let's just laugh about this together, please. Let's just blame Grandpa for this." I was off-balance.

"Oh, honey," she said quietly. "I'm not upset with you. Never."

I took a minute to think about what she was saying.

Then it hit me, like a dented truck: I was the victim, sure, but Mom was, too. Her father raised her to be fearful of everything, just as she had done to me. I couldn't be angry at her; we were the same person.

Realizing that truth didn't help any, though. I was still

angry. Mom raised me—albeit unintentionally—to think I couldn't make it without her. And there was no fighting it.

Just the thought of trying to go one step without her felt like everything I'd written down in my yellow notepad had come true.

I was alone. And no one was coming to get me.

Santa Monica. Again. 2004

The greatest thing about graduating from college was that it meant I got to move back down south to Los Angeles.

Rather than spending the year adrift like most of my college peers were doing, backpacking across Western Europe or just being generally lazy, I'd chosen to immediately attend a part-time Sport Management graduate program at California State University Long Beach. It hadn't even occurred to me that I'd do anything else after Santa Barbara. I'd minored in Sport Management at UCSB and had become fascinated with behind-the-scenes work within the athletic space. Sports was all I knew, and I decided I wanted to work for a professional sports team after I graduated. Maybe the Dodgers, which was Dad's favorite. I applied to three prestigious graduate programs but was sold on Long Beach when I learned it was only a 35-minute drive from my parents' house in Santa Monica. Without traffic. It was magical moving back in with them. I felt whole again.

Charles and I were still together when I graduated college, but he elected to go the popular five-year academic route, so he stayed at school to finish up. Thinking about him and the friends I'd left behind in Santa Barbara made me question my choice to leave. As much as I enjoyed being back home, I wasn't sure I wanted to work in sports, and I felt trapped.

During my second week of graduate school I'd had enough of the internal turmoil, so I decided I would talk to Donna, the Sport Management Program Manager, about leaving CSU Long Beach entirely.

Class started at 6:00 p.m. as it always had, and the first break wasn't until 7:30 p.m. I could barely sit still in class, playing my forthcoming conversation with Donna over and over again in my head.

Finally. 7:30 p.m.

I charged out of my desk and headed for Donna. "So I think," I told her, meekly. "How would it work if I needed to stop the program?" I'd spent the afternoon rehearsing what I was going to say, but when I finally had the gall to speak with Donna I could barely cobble together a sentence.

Donna was a kind woman in her late 40s, and she'd graduated from the program herself years before, so she was extra enthusiastic about guiding new students. She had a pronounced Southern accent, which, having spent my entire life in California, charmed me whenever she spoke.

She gave me a knowing smile when I shared my concerns, as if she'd been given this sloppy speech before, and suggested we talk in the hall, where we'd have more privacy.

I continued, "I might go back to Santa Barbara for more classes."

While missing Charles may have triggered the new chapter of academic chaos I was creating, wanting to take other classes was also a factor in my growing uncertainty about Sport Management.

On my last day of undergrad I'd walked through the hall of the Sociology building at UCSB and into an elevator, where a simple white bulletin caught my attention just as the doors were closing. It read "Minor In Magazine Writing."

Something inside of me clicked when I saw it—I'd always enjoyed writing, but as a Sociology/Sport Management student I never needed to take a proper writing class—yet with only a week before graduation it made no sense to even inquire about the program, so I talked myself down from the curiosity ledge as soon as I spotted it. In my mind's eye I hit the rewind button—walking backward down a hallway I'd just left, reading a sign, going into a brand new department to learn about a brand new area of study—it was all out of the question. I had to move forward and graduate, because that's what sensible people did.

But I should've inquired about writing that day when I saw the bulletin, because now, knee-deep in a graduate program focused on sports, all I could think about was writing. Writing was my safe place. It's where I could pour myself onto a page, and understand who I really was. I had to become a writer.

Now.

Now.

NOW.

She leaned her right shoulder against the wall. "It's perfectly normal to feel this way, but you shouldn't make a rash decision."

I hated her tone. It felt judgmental, and parental, and not at all what I wanted from her.

But then she continued. "There's no problem putting your enrollment on hold, but you should spend more time thinking about it first."

I exhaled in relief. I didn't know what Donna *thought* she said, but I interpreted it in the best way possible. Donna was okay with me leaving graduate school. She was okay with me following my gut and doing what felt right.

My parents were already asleep by the time I got home from class, so I went straight to my room and excitedly plotted my return to Santa Barbara in between trips to the restroom to deal with anxiety-induced stomach aches. No attack, though. Just lingering anxiety.

Since completing treatment with Dr. Schwinn, I'd grown accustomed to what anxiety felt like, and learned that trying to stop it—or fearing it—is what would turn a tight throat sensation into a high-speed attack. Saying "hello" to anxiety when it reared its head was slightly manageable, and acknowledging early on that it would prevent me from sleeping was our "agreement." Anxiety ran the show, and as long as I allowed it to remain the alpha, I would be okay.

While I didn't fall asleep until 5:00 a.m., when 9:00 a.m. hit I ran into a spare bedroom in the house as though I was operating on a full night's sleep. My bedroom didn't have a lock on the door, but that one did. I locked it immediately, said "hello" to anxiety, and called the admissions department at UCSB and redacted my diploma.

"I'd like to re-enroll in school, please," I happily told the woman on the other end of the line. I could hardly sit still. I needed to use the bathroom again, but I held back as best I could. This was more important.

"There's a credit cap, but let's see here," she paused while she typed on her computer. "Looks like you can take up to 10 more. That's three classes."

"Perfect," I said.

It took me 20 minutes to undo four years of being an on-track student.

She gave me my online credentials and I hung up, quickly booting up my parents' Dell computer in the guest room. *Hold your horses, anxiety.* I had to do one more thing. I logged into the UCSB system and signed up for Magazine Writing 101. Spot

89 out of 90. *Yes.*

I sprinted to the bathroom practically bubbling over with joy, and returned a minute later to call Deena and Cara, two of my former UCSB roommates. They were an academic year younger than me and were now seniors. We'd lived together my last year in school and they had become two of my best friends. They were sharing a one-bedroom apartment for their senior year—everyone shared bedrooms in Santa Barbara. One of the things I'd decided the night prior was that it made perfect sense to move back to Santa Barbara and live with them. I was going to become a magazine writer and I couldn't wait to tell them about it.

"Why would you do that?" Deena asked when I told her the plan over the phone. "You already graduated." She wasn't the least bit excited by my plan.

I needed her on my side. "I don't want to work in sports anymore. I want to become a writer." The knots in my stomach became thick, slowly churning and twisting.

"You're just doing this to be with Charles."

She didn't get it. She was one of my best friends, why didn't she understand that I was coming back to school to become a writer?

I was deaf to her objections. "I could move into your and Cara's apartment in a few weeks."

"But Bek, we have a one-bedroom apartment and it's really tight as it is," she said, still not getting it. They did have a small apartment, but it wasn't uncommon for even three roommates to share a room in Santa Barbara. You just needed to be creative about bunking.

And creative I was.

That afternoon I frantically mapped out a layout of how we could squeeze three twin beds into their room. I drew everything to scale and had arrows going in all directions, explaining which slash mark and which rectangle shape belonged to who. Cara and Deena's beds would go on the north-south walls, and I'd go perpendicularly. The money we'd save by splitting the rent three ways would go toward new bed frames with plenty of storage space. Once I had the blueprints just right I redrew them onto a fresh piece of paper and put the drawing in the mail so Deena could see how doable it really was.

Confident that I'd sway her, I moved my focus to my parents. I approached them slowly; methodically. If I'd been able to keep it from them longer I would have, but the tangled braid of nerves in my stomach was tearing me up. I was drowning in my anxiety—I had to tell them.

"You know how much I've always enjoyed writing," I said when I found them in the living room together.

"Sure, sweetie," Mom said, smiling at me earnestly. "Do you want to take a UCLA Extension class in writing?" she blurted, three steps ahead of me. Her brain moved faster than mine. "We just got the catalog in the mail."

"I want to do more than that," I said firmly. "I think." I

paused a minute before finishing. "I sort of re-enrolled at UCSB so that I could pursue a Magazine Writing minor I just learned about." I let out a loud burp. The release felt good.

"Beki, you're just being emotional," Mom said. "You do this all the time, but you can't go back to the school you already left." She looked at Dad, who was lying on the couch with his eyes half shut, hands folded serenely at his chest, hoping that we'd finish up so he could get back to his nap.

Dad mumbled quietly from his spot on the couch. "Beki, you're the one that wanted to go to this graduate program. If you're unhappy in it, then we don't need to force you to do it." His voice was monotone, as if he were trying to not wake himself by producing too loud a volume. Before I could thank Dad for his support, he added, "Now please, I'd like to take a nap I didn't sleep at all last night."

If my father was to be believed, he hadn't had a decent night's sleep in 15 years.

I felt the need to celebrate.

I got in the car and drove to the big newsstand on San Vicente Boulevard so that I could buy my two favorite magazines: *Lucky* and *Jane*. I spent the night tearing them apart and stapling my favorite pages to the wall.

I was going to become a magazine writer.

Deena called. She got my sketches in the mail. When I answered the phone I half-hoped she'd be cheering on the other end of the line. My return would inject their apartment with more life. But instead she seemed disappointed in me, as though I'd asked her to loan me money. "I don't think it's going to work," she said. "And you were so excited about your graduate program. Are you sure you want to leave it?"

Still, I pushed back. "Yes, I've given this tons of thought." I obviously hadn't. "And squeezing in three people will totally work. We can fit in the bedroom no problem." The plan was fool-proof and I was one of her best friends. She had to cave.

"I'm sorry, I hear that you want to come back to school, and I love you and obviously Cara and I want you to visit us every weekend if you can, but you can't live here."

I became even more obsessive about the idea, drawing new bedroom floor plans to share with Deena. *A pull-out couch, of course! Pure genius.* Then I researched space-saving drawers that could hide behind the couch. No one would know. I thought of new angles for the couch, ways to give myself some privacy, and ripped a photo of a privacy screen out of a home decor catalogue that would be perfect in Deena's apartment.

I felt exuberant. I'd turned all that negativity around and figured out an even better way to do the thing I knew I was supposed to do all along: spend a fifth year in Santa Barbara with my best friends, learning to become a writer. My aunt

Charlotte was an extremely successful television comedy writer, working on shows like *The Mary Tyler Moore Show*, *The Bob Newhart Show*, and *Rhoda*. She was the first woman showrunner—a true trailblazer for female writers—why did it take me so long to figure out that this was the career path to follow? It was in my blood.

Who cared what other people thought? I did things differently than most people, and I'd come to terms with that.

When Deena called—again—and said that she loved me—again—but that I could not live on their couch, I threw in the towel. Not on my dream of writing, but on going backward. Living in the in-between was smothering me—I had to pull the trigger and make a decision.

I called the Admissions Department at UCSB and said nevermind. I'd made a mess and annoyed my best friend, but I didn't need Santa Barbara to become a writer.

All I needed was a computer.

The Workforce, 2005

A year later, I interviewed at *LA Livin'* magazine in Los Angeles. I'd never interviewed for anything other than a sports job before. The rules for those were pretty simple and always the same: wear ill-fitting khaki pants and don't try to one-up any of the women that work there by doing things like carrying an expensive handbag or wearing high heels that show off your calves. I learned that at the Los Angeles Clippers, when a returning intern schooled me on the NBA's unwritten interview dress code.

"Don't try and look too made up or wear high-end labels, you can't be prettier than the women that work here," she advised. "In fact, don't try and look pretty at all."

An interview for a job at a magazine, though, was completely different. I had to be trendy, but not too trendy. Casual, but not too casual.

I tried on everything I owned before settling on a pair of Seven jeans with pink rhinestones on the butt, a Ramones band T-shirt I'd purchased from Urban Outfitters over a decade prior, and a baby pink blazer with the sleeves permanently rolled up.

My brother Danny was dating a girl named Jessica in Los Angeles, and over a holiday dinner she mentioned she had just been hired as the Associate Publisher at a slick new magazine called *LA Livin'*, a high-end glossy whose purpose was to report on everything and everyone expensive. Jessica loved my brother so she helped me get an interview. Even though I had no experience or much formal schooling to warrant my getting a job at a magazine, I eagerly pursued it.

Once I settled on my uncomfortably sparkly interview outfit I drove to the Coffee Bean & Tea Leaf on Beverly Drive in Beverly Hills to meet with *LA Livin'*s CEO, Matt. I took a seat by the window and fiddled around with my résumé, trying not to stain it with the sweat from my palms. Pre-interview jitters never brought on a panic attack because the anxiety was warranted.

Matt arrived 20 minutes late, wearing camouflage pants and a thin black T-shirt. I immediately felt stupid for wearing so much pink. It wasn't "me."

Matt asked me a few questions, mainly focusing on the cool happenings in town and my knowledge thereof. I spent the entire time staring at him confused as to how he owned a magazine. He wasn't that much older than me.

After listening to Matt talk about what the magazine

would look like—it hadn't launched in Los Angeles yet—I discovered quickly that working at *LA Livin'* would be my first glimpse into the affluent lifestyle that I'd spent nearly a decade trying to deny. I was embarrassingly unfamiliar with it. I knew a lot about sport franchises and handling professional athletes, and even more about operational gymnasium minutiae like how to pull out the bleachers manually when the motor was stuck, but none of that would be of any use at a magazine—at least not at this magazine. Matt told me the magazine was set to launch in nine months, and if I got the job I would be the office assistant/receptionist. I wanted a writing job, but there was an adult voice inside of me that recognized that I had no experience writing. I'd have to prove myself and work my way out of reception.

When a woman named Diane called me a week later to tell me I got the job, I stopped breathing. Writing for magazines had only been something I started thinking about recently, and I never even had the chance to learn how to do it correctly, but the stars were aligning.

The position paid me a whopping $36,000 a year plus a brand new Sony laptop and a BlackBerry that I'd soon learn would never stop buzzing. And because I was going to earn a salary, I told Mom and Dad that I was ready to move out.

My parents were in awe. And I was too.

LA Livin' occupied the sleekest office space on the Sunset Strip, and because of our crafty trade deals with advertisers (we gave them ad space in our magazine in exchange for free products), it was decked out with over 30 flat-screen TVs, a state-of-the-art nightclub sound system, a full bar stocked with booze I'd never heard of, like Triple Sex Death Vodka, and a half dozen lapdogs that scampered freely around the office like we were running a doggy day care.

The dogs were paid for. And they shit everywhere.

It was an absolutely gorgeous workplace and I felt like a woman of power each morning as I stepped inside. Even if I just answered the phone.

I spent the first three months as a run-of-the-mill office assistant, answering calls, sending stacks of mail in flat-rate envelopes to potential advertisers, driving Matt's various luxury SUVs to get detailed at a private car wash located in the basement of our building's parking structure, and occasionally taking his girlfriend's satin bustiers to the dry cleaners. I was younger than everyone else in the office, so I rarely did anything other than sit at my desk or run errands.

The magazine was going to focus on fashion, beauty, and entertainment, and since we were located in Los Angeles, articles were going to profile the cool up-and-comers that lived in our city. It was going to be a stunning magazine. I was impressed by it.

One day our sales team asked me to join them at lunch, and I jumped at the chance, briskly walking to see our

Office Manager Sammy so I could let him know. Sammy had an enormously wide, friendly smile that contradicted his stern personality. I'd never actually gone out to lunch before. I typically ate at my desk, splashing my monitor with droplets of balsamic vinaigrette anytime my to-go salad was prepared by someone with a heavy hand.

"Would it be alright if I joined the sales team at lunch?" I asked softly. "They just invited me." I looked in the direction of the sales team hoping for some sort of brotherly cheer, but they were all busy at their desks.

Sammy slammed his phone down on his desk and glared at me as if I'd just interrupted his conference call with the President. "I need you in your chair," he said, annoyed. "You think you can just leave whenever you want?"

I instantly had my first hot flash, 30 years earlier than anticipated. My armpits, my back, my hair were all sweating.

He leaned forward to grab his phone again and punched in a number. Back to the President, I assumed. Quickly he added, "How about you just do your job, Rebecca?" I took the dialing as an indication that our conversation was over.

I went back to my desk completely mortified. I knew he was a jerk, but I'd never had anyone confront me like that before. *Was I wrong to ask about leaving for lunch,* I wondered. I stared at the wall and zoned out. If I'd allowed myself to actually be in that moment, I would have started crying and I knew better than to let that happen at work.

My coworkers eventually got up to leave for lunch and as they scooted past my desk, I shook my head and looked down, embarrassed. They understood what that meant. "What a dick," one of them said.

Suddenly I felt someone's presence. Sammy was standing at my desk. I thought perhaps he came to apologize and I could still catch up with the sales team. He pulled a $20 bill out of his wallet, crumbled it, and flicked it onto my laptop as if it was trash.

"We're out of coffee. Buy a bag."

I went out to buy the coffee and called Mom to cry. "You are tough," she told me. "It's hard to be an assistant, but remember this moment because one day you will be the boss." While her advice was calming, it wasn't enough to keep me settled.

Tension at work never let up—if it wasn't Sammy making me feel small, it was our Operations Manager Diane hovering over me like a drone. Anytime I left my desk, even if it was to get coffee supplies for the office or to pick up Matt's car from the detailer, she would email me on my BlackBerry with curt messages: "Where are you? You're not at your desk and I had to answer the phone."

And it seemed like the earlier I got to work in the morning, the later everyone else came in. They'd stay out late at night and hit up the Hollywood club scene with potential advertisers, buying them bottles and perhaps recreational drugs until the advertisers were ready to head home. Sammy, Diane, and the other staffers would stroll in really late—sometimes at 11:00 a.m.—and ask me to buy them cans of Red Bull or call the parking structure on La Cienega Boulevard because their cars got locked in the night before and they needed to get them out. And the worst part about those sort of requests was that they always came in piecemeal. Diane would never tell me which parking garage she left her car in, or that she hated regular Red Bull and only drank sugar-free, so it always took me twice as long to accomplish menial tasks. I had become the office's ugly drudge. I was Anne Hathaway in *The Devil Wears Prada*, but instead of working at the illustrious *Vogue*, I was working for party kids that just happened to run a magazine.

One day Matt came up to me at my desk and told me he wanted computer speakers. He didn't remember the model, but he said they were silver and about "this big," demonstrating their size with his hands, and said they sold them at the Apple store at The Grove.

"Do you remember anything else about them?" I asked.

He was scrolling through messages on his Blackberry but stopped and looked up at me. "Huh?"

I exhaled through my nose disparagingly. "The speakers, anything else you remember?"

"Do you need me to do this?"

"Nope, got it."

I clenched my butt cheeks, holding back my attitude. I

couldn't understand him. Matt was the guy that hired me. I thought it was because he saw something promising in me, but I realized what he saw was someone that would cower to him. Why would he belittle me over something as unnecessary as speakers? He was young—only 30—but I put him on a pedestal, too nervous to stand up for myself at 23.

I called the Apple store and ordered three different pairs of speakers so that I could return whichever "this big" ones Matt didn't want. It was the only solution I could come up with, and finding solutions to problems was becoming my strong suit. My bosses at the magazine seemed to get off on making me feel irrelevant, so there was never an opportunity to seek help when it came to problem-solving. I had to come up with answers on the fly.

When the speakers arrived at our Los Angeles office later that week, Matt was in another city on business, where he bought completely different speakers from a completely different brand and sent me an email to tell me about it. It said, "Got speakers on my own. I don't understand why it was so hard for you. It took me 20 minutes." His emails never had "hellos" or "goodbyes," just fast messages that were obviously written on his BlackBerry with the intent of being condescending.

I continued to call Mom when these things happened, so with her sage advice and my desire to become a writer, I found a way to tolerate being treated so poorly. Part of the toleration stemmed from biweekly therapy appointments I'd attend after work.

Six months after I was hired, the magazine was ready to launch and they finally hired an editor. I could tell after meeting her that she was desperate for an assistant. I knew nothing about grammar and sentence structure since I didn't take any journalism courses in college, but I loved to write. I'd spent the last year in undergrad writing a lot of poetry and performing my spoken word pieces at various open mic nights throughout Santa Barbara and Los Angeles—before spoken word landed on HBO and became abhorrently mainstream. I found it embarrassing to participate in once it became popular.

Writing poetry was always something I did privately, and performing on stage to a receptive audience that wanted to feel something was an addictive rush. It was the payoff to the sadness I felt when I wrote. But once the audience members at Greenway Court Theatre on Fairfax Avenue in Los Angeles started sharing the room with people that were attending spoken word because it was trendy, I lost my desire to share my work. On stage I could bleed my feelings out, yell and gesticulate in ways that came naturally. I needed the people on the receiving end to want to feel me fully. And an audience of tourists or trend-seekers wasn't appealing. So I stopped performing.

And I didn't miss it one bit once I became a real staffer at a magazine. Even one that just answered phones.

Laura, *LA Livin's* new Managing Editor, had only $1,000 a month to spend on freelancers, which, during our first meeting, she called "fucking ridiculous given how much money the company was spending on partying."

I offered to write articles for her for free and because she had no other alternative she said yes. All I had to do was convince Sammy that'd I'd be able to track down missing cars and answer the phone while contributing to the magazine. By now I knew how to work Sammy. I built up his ego, pretending he was a person I could stomach, and then politely persuaded him that I could do both jobs.

The first article I wrote for Laura was about a new massive sport megaplex being built in Downtown Los Angeles, called L.A. Live. Because of my connections in the sport world, I knew about it before anyone else did, and I had an immediate "in." The story closed in at around 1,000 words and included an interview with one of the developers of the project. I had no idea what I was doing or how to conduct an interview—I didn't even own an audio recorder—so I was relieved when, after calling the developer to schedule an in-person interview, his assistant told me he was only available for email questions.

Months later I was sitting in a small conference room with Laura and Matt. Laura put the meeting on the calendar. We were hopefully going to discuss the possibility of a new position at the company for me. I'd been doing such a good job at my dual role as office assistant and in-house writer, and even volunteered for the magazine pages that no one wanted to work on, like the Party Scene, which was a miserable collage of photos and captions that you had to get right otherwise advertisers would be upset. From across the table, Laura gave me a nod that signified good things were going to come out of this meeting.

I sat on my hands to control my nerves.

Laura and I sat in silence until Matt finished typing an email on his phone, then he cracked open a Red Bull and looked at me.

"Yeah, so I'm making you the Editorial Assistant, I'll need to hire another assistant to replace your spot at reception. I know you don't want that job, you want to be a writer," he said, sounding bored. He took a sip from his can and set it back down. "You'll work under Laura now, which means the magazine should look twice as good now that there are two people on the editorial team. So, if you fuck things up you'll be fired."

I let it soak in before answering. Not exactly how I envisioned adult promotions happening. It felt more like a threat than an advancement, but I wanted to be a writer. So I nodded. I wanted to play.

"Thank you so much."

~~~~~~

From: Laura Desal [mailto: Laura@LaLivin.com]
Sent: Monday, February 27, 2006 4:52 PM
To: Rebecca@LaLivin.com
Subject: Assignment – TAN

So that Matt can have a free golden tan year round
we must do a profile on Golden Performance
Airbrush Tanning.

Please assign it out and ask that the writer contact the dimwit that owns the company for
quotes...and to make her feel special.

~~~~~~

Laura had long blonde, luminescent hair that matched her
personality, and while she was actually an amazing writer,
she was always on edge and that made me uncomfortable.
I never knew when she was going to snap. Sometimes she'd
send me nasty messages at night critiquing the quality of
my work or telling me that emails I had sent to people earlier in the day were "complete crap." Other times she'd
message me while she was working remotely to make sure
that I was actually working because she just had a feeling
that I wasn't. Sometimes I defended myself and sometimes
I let it slide—neither technique was effective. She was overworked and underpaid and I was her minion. But because I
legitimately respected her, her harsh words hurt more than
anything Sammy or Matt could have ever said.

Things took a dramatic shift at work the day Matt went

to coffee with a woman named Annalise. Because Matt was a guy with things to do and messages to type, he decided right there on the spot that this mysterious Annalise should be our new Editor-in-Chief. He first announced the news to Laura, who then sent me a personal email over the weekend detailing all the ways in which Annalise was not qualified for the job.

"She's a user, I've worked with her before. And she's also not even an editor. The woman has never published an article in her life. Not even for a school paper."

Then Laura sent the same email to Matt. The subject line read: The Downfall of *LA Livin'*.

It didn't take long before Laura and Annalise started to battle over everything; Laura wanted the magazine to focus on cool locals, and Annalise wanted us to profile West Hollywood cafe owners that offered to give us free food in exchange for press coverage. I obviously sided with Laura—while I'd had no editorial experience it felt weird to give press to businesses that gave the heads of our company free chopped salad—but I kept those opinions inside the walls of the editorial office. I wasn't ready to face off with Annalise. She was short, but she was scary.

I wasn't the least bit surprised the morning that Laura was fired. Matt called her into the big conference room and Laura yelled a bunch as she shamed Annalise and fought for her job. Later that night, Laura sent me a note from her personal email. I knew it was going to be a bad one, but I read it anyway:

From: Laura Desal [mailto: LauraD@ ▮▮▮▮▮▮▮▮▮]
Sent: Friday, November 10, 2006 11:39 PM
To: Rebecca@LaLivin.com
Subject: Laughable

This was always Annalise's plan. She will continue to eliminate anyone that she can't keep under her thumb. I can't believe you didn't quit after they fired me. I brought you into the editorial department. Why would you want to stay there and work with those people? You're a sheep.

Even though I lost respect for you today, you no longer work under me, so maybe we can be friends.

When I finished Laura's email my heart crashed to the floor. I'd failed my boss somehow. I had so much respect for her passion to both the magazine and to the craft of writing, how had I done such a bad job at earning her respect? Why did she call me a sheep? Did she think I was a terrible writer too? The idea that I'd failed to impress my editor made me want to rip my hair out. Writing was everything to me, and I was still growing. I had so much to learn, and now I had no one to learn it from because my boss had just been fired.

I dialed my parents and asked if I could spend the night.

LA Livin' magazine, 2007

Mary was beautiful and spoke quietly, sometimes punctuating thoughts with graceful hand movements that were ballerina-like.

She'd previously been the Editor of *YM* magazine in Manhattan, and talked about everyone in the media world in a way that made me envy her. While people living in Hollywood typically rambled on about their famous D-list neighbors and meaningless celebrity run-ins at Whole Foods, Mary spoke eloquently of her editorial cronies; she was the real deal. She was sincere. I cherished every bit of information she threw my way and I couldn't believe that *LA Livin'* talked her into being our replacement editor after Laura vanished. I couldn't understand how they convinced a real journalist to spearhead our department.

She was everything my old editor Laura wasn't: kind and supportive of my work. Even though Mary challenged me, there was never any sense of competition between us. Mary was already good at what she did, so she only wanted me to become better. It was authentic.

Sometimes after work I'd sneakily take Mary's drafts home and read them over and over—she could practically paint pictures with her words, even if they were about a stupid new body slimming treatment that Annalise asked her to write about. I wanted to learn the way she ebbed and flowed. But even with Mary's warm approach to me and the office, it didn't take long for my unhappiness at work and anxiety to resurface. Panic was no longer something that was reserved for big moves or new sleepovers; it was a round-the-clock disturbance that clung to me like a shadow.

"This office gives me a headache," I told Mary one afternoon while flipping through the features section of *Lucky* magazine and massaging my temples. Headaches were something I'd been dealing with more frequently since working there. They didn't always lead to a tidal wave of emotion, but almost every panic attack kicked off with a headache. I believed I could reduce the likelihood that a stressful situation would turn into more by giving myself a light temple massage.

Mary had been at the company six months and was beginning to feel the same way I did about everyone there, so I was comfortable opening up to her.

"Go to New York," she'd tell me. "You belong there."

Next to my new behavioral therapist, who I started seeing after anxiety in the workplace became unmanageable and I once again couldn't sleep at night. She was the only other person in Southern California that encouraged me to wash my hands of *LA Livin'* and the town I called home.

My parents didn't understand the office politics either, but they wanted me to stick it out.

"This is a really important learning experience for you," Dad would say when I would tell him how angry everyone was making me. "It's important to learn how to react to these things without emotion."

His advice annoyed me—it felt antiquated—so I'd thank him for listening and either hang up the phone, or leave my parents' house and drive back to my apartment.

Mary and I were the only two normal employees at the magazine. We didn't come in hungover or have temper tantrums, like many staffers. But this also meant that most staffers disliked us. Especially *LA Livin'*'s Nightlife Manager, Peter. I didn't know much about the publishing world before I joined *LA Livin'*, but I sure as heck did not know that magazines kept nightlife managers on staff.

Peter was a mid-30-year-old tan-aholic who spent much of the day across the street at Sunset Tan, getting sprayed or lying in tanning beds—he liked to mix it up, much like the way a marathoner might change up his or her running shoes in between long training sessions. Peter was fascinating to look at, with cheeks so pronounced they could've been implants, but they were most likely the result of good genetics. He was the type of guy that seemed like he'd been handsome for awhile. If Brad Pitt was a cartoonish EDM raver he'd be Peter.

Peter frolicked around in loud outfits and bragged about having threesomes at Sunset Tan. You never wanted to believe his stories because they were too preposterous, but then a few hours later blonde twins would come into the office giggling and looking for him.

At his best, Peter was coked out and manic; at his worst, he was coked out and manic, but he was invaluable to *LA Livin'* because he provided Matt, Sammy, and the rest of the untouchable management team with access to a nightlife they'd never be privy to elsewhere.

Peter, with his impressive surplus of neon Gucci loafers, knew Hollywood.

People were drawn to Peter because he promoted some of the hottest clubs in town. He was the nightlife right-hand man to one of the most influential event producers in Hollywood, and he thought very little of me and Mary, even if he did lift up his T-shirts to share his highbrow designer underwear with us.

If it weren't for Peter's palpable hatred of me, I may have never quit.

~~~~~~~~

"They literally specialize in late-night hot dog delivery. I can't believe we have to profile them," Mary complained.

She and I were in the middle of groaning about a friend of Matt's that worked at a food delivery service store on Sunset Boulevard when Peter appeared. He normally came in for an hour or two in between tanning sessions. Sometimes he'd drive into the office on a miniature red motorcycle and park it right in the center of our office, purely to cause a commotion.

Peter burst into the editorial office with his Yorkie dog attached to a hot pink leash.

"You guys fucking fucked everything up! I told you that the Diesel party had to be the last party page in the magazine and you screwed it up!" he shouted while his cheeks twitched.

Two years in the editorial department and I was still managing the Party Scene section, and once Peter joined the company the pages became much more complicated. It was no longer about correctly identifying names of guests—I had to make sure that all the important nightlife people and models were included, too. It was hard. They all looked the same to me. In the photos, gaggles of blonde girls with perfectly proportioned bodies hung onto the arms of grossly older men in beige blazers and tattoo-inspired T-shirts. Who could tell the difference between a girl named Candy and a girl named Brandy? It was a time-consuming duty, and once I put together the pages, Peter would have to sign off on everything and make sure that the right events and the right brands appeared. Perhaps the only real job responsibility of a Nightlife Manager.

The task of getting Peter to approve things was even more difficult than the work itself because he was impossible to track down.

He pulled his BlackBerry from his flared jeans. "I'm texting Matt, I'm telling him what you guys did. You put this guy Matt hates right, smack in our magazine. We're never going to be able to partner with Hive nightclub because you fucking put in this ugly cheesy douchebag," he said while furiously typing away. "How do you spell 'dismantle'?"

I looked up at Mary.

I didn't even know who Peter was talking about. But he was right. I did put the wrong party and the wrong guy into the magazine, and it was too late to change it. Those pages had already gone to the printer.

"Don't text Matt," I said.

"Too late, man," Peter said with a laugh.

I gulped the loudest gulp I'd ever heard myself gulp. I knew that the moment Matt looked at his phone he would come barreling in. My palms were thick with sweat.

"You were supposed to approve those pages, that's your job. Just like it's your job to come into the office and write that monthly column of yours about partying," Mary said sternly.

She always had my back, but rarely raised her voice.

We gave Peter a full page in the magazine every month so he could write under his alter-ego Dirk Landers and satirically rant about how to hook up with chicks, eat for free, and party in L.A. Or at least I thought it was supposed to be satirical.

I could feel the blood in my veins surge wildly, and looked down at the floor to focus my attention on something finite, like a scuff mark.

Or a dog poop stain.

"No, don't even. This is so bad," Peter went on.

My heart beat faster. I wiped my palms against my legs to absorb the sweat, but they were slippery against the fabric of my jeans. I wanted to diffuse the situation and make Peter disappear but I couldn't think of anything to say.

Peter wasn't finished with us. He had more to add. "I don't have fucking time to do this shit. This is your fucking shit, I run the scene, I have important meetings to take and I have to look good, bitches. Whatever, you two are idiots and now we look so bad."

Peter's tongue grazed his bottom lip, running back and forth like a starved dog at mealtime. "Matt is not going to be happy when he sees that you put these ugly people in his magazine. Do you guys even go out? Fat people don't come to my clubs, so they shouldn't be in my magazine! They'd never get into my clubs because they're fucking Las Vegas trash." Peter swung our glass door open and pranced out like a deer. His Yorkie followed, trotting to keep up.

My body was flushed, partly with anger and partly with

uncertainty because surviving *LA Livin'* had nothing to do with being good at my job. I had to stay under the radar.

"I emailed Peter at least three times to come look at the final proofs for our nightlife pages. And we didn't make the call to push Diesel to front-of-book," I said to Mary nervously. Peter was the one that screwed it up.

"Stop," she demanded, slamming her palm into the desk. This wasn't the first time Peter had a hissy fit, or the first time that photos of parties dictated our workflow. "We have to close the book tomorrow, we don't have time for this."

"Fine. I'm gonna step outside and get some air."

Outside I found an intimate space next to the building. A point at which the windows inverted, making a sharp V-shape along the façade. It was for style. For me, it provided a safe space to take deep breaths and cry. If I could just let out a few ugly tears I could regain control of my irregular heartbeat.

I called my therapist and asked if she had time to see me that evening.

———

At 5:58 p.m. I pulled up to the curb of Dr. Trafest's sprawling home and shut off the engine. Between the time I'd called her and the time I'd arrived at her home, I'd lost interest in the appointment. I wanted to go home and crawl into bed; talking felt like a chore. But I didn't have the nerve to call and cancel, so I put the car in park and got out.

Her home always looked unoccupied, with just a few porch lights on to illuminate the front walkway. I took the driveway entrance as always, bypassing the home entirely and heading directly into the backyard, where I walked up a flight of stairs and let myself into a back guest house.

The waiting room was bare, per usual, with classical music quietly playing on a dual tape deck. It made the space feel more haunted than it needed to. I knew that the beautiful strains of violins were supposed to calm people, but they made me restless. Each song bled into the next.

At 6:01 p.m. I grew jittery, bouncing in my seat by clenching my butt cheeks at an intermittent pace. I wanted to leave and go home. I considered how I'd sneak out. I wondered if she knew I'd already arrived or if she was inside the main house.

Before I could plot a proper exit, she opened up the sliding doors to her office and gave me her usual modest smile, an indication that I should follow her inside for our session.

~~~~~~~~

When I showed up for work the next morning, I was surprised to see Peter sitting in the workspace adjacent to my office. He looked completely different than he had the day before, wearing a wrinkled T-shirt and nervously chewing on a large ball of masking tape that he'd made himself. He was deeply focused on the ball of tape when I walked in. A strip of neon trim peeked out above his waistband—the glow-in-the-dark underwear he showed me the previous week.

"What are you chewing on?" I asked.

"My tape ball," he murmured, still with his head down. "It's my tape ball." His lips barely opened as he answered me. "Tape. Tape." He said it hurriedly.

I laughed to myself and sat down at my desk. The scary Peter from yesterday who got me so worked up that I had to go to therapy was now just a wounded bird, taking refuge near my office and hiding from whomever or whatever it was that was haunting him. For a moment I felt bad for him.

Peter looked as though he hadn't slept all night, and the fact that he was awake at 10:00 a.m. and in the *LA Livin'* office was supremely bizarre. I was about to ask him if he needed anything—coffee, water, perhaps another roll of masking tape—when he started furiously itching his nose with the tape ball. I stopped myself, remembering who I was dealing with.

Peter wasn't here to talk or looking to apologize about yesterday, he was coked out of his mind. He probably slept here. I got out of my chair, walked over to the door separating my office from the communal workspace he was seated in, and shut it.

"I have a call with the hot dog delivery guy," I said.

~~~~~~

As my anxiety at work got worse, I spent more time at Dr. Trafest's. My obsessions with death morphed into a new obsession: the need to escape. I felt trapped in my life. Not just at the magazine but in Los Angeles. I'd never seen my hometown through this grossly affected lens before, and it made me hate myself. Maybe it was the judgment I felt from Peter and Matt for never being a stereotypical party girl that hogged restroom stalls in order to do lines of coke when people obviously just had to pee, but I knew one thing for sure: I wanted to get out of Los Angeles and away from everything *LA Livin'*. It was breaking me and sending me back to my college mindset where I felt out of control.

I frequently shared this with my parents. Dad was particularly saddened. He had no experience dealing with anxiety and the fact that I wasn't cured yet—the fact that I was still so scared all of the time—broke his heart. He and Mom offered to pay for all of my therapy sessions, which I allowed.

"Have you given any more thought to whether you're ready to leave the magazine?" Dad finally asked one night when I joined them at their house for dinner. "What does your therapist think about the environment you're in?"

Finally! He stopped with the parental speech about this being a learning experience and was actually listening to me.

Sometimes I felt like looping my parents in with every detail of what happened in the office and in therapy. They were the only people that had the tolerance to listen to all of the repetitive stories. Other times, though, I was angry with Mom for raising me to be so weak so I wouldn't tell her anything out of spite.

I didn't answer Dad; instead, I diverted the conversation completely. "Maybe I'll finally go to New York," I said. "Everyone has always said I belong there."

New York was the only other state I had spent a significant amount of time in since my grandparents lived there, so it made sense, and it was something Mary was always talking to me about.

Dad's expression was non-committal. I wondered if he hadn't heard me. "You're a late bloomer," he finally said, calmly. "I support you if you want to try it. It would be like you finally went away to college, just a little bit later than most."

While it was meant to be a joke I hung onto that sentence. I had never gone away to college. Not far away, at least.

Mom looked at him, then looked at me. "Well, New York is hard and dangerous," she added. "I don't know if you are ready for that. You don't want to know the kind of stuff that happened to me there."

I rolled my eyes.

It was exactly the response I knew I'd get from her. Mom would never want me to move to New York. As a child this would have certainly steered me the other way—I couldn't do anything without Mom's approval—but at 25, something about her disapproval excited me.

"You're so predictable, Mom," I said. I couldn't believe the words that came out of my mouth.

Defiant.

Mean, even.

But I wanted to prove her wrong.

Dr. Trafest taught me a lot about dependency and helped me see how much I relied on Mom for security.

I felt like a person with two identities: the helpless young girl who cried to Mom and needed her permission in order to survive, and the educated young adult in therapy that saw Girl 1 as a pathetic child with no identity.

As soon as I heard Mom say I shouldn't move, I decided I was absolutely going to. I had to. The anxiety I would feel from moving seemed like it would be more manageable than the anxiety I felt from staying in L.A. As long as Dr. Trafest was behind me. I still wasn't running the Rebecca show, but there was no way I'd let Mom remain my operator.

I was too frightened to travel to Manhattan alone, so I decided I'd only go if I could talk someone into traveling with me.

Midtown Manhattan, 2007

I took a cab uptown to Times Square for an informational interview with Condé Nast Publishing. Informational interviews were something Mary taught me about. It's when the applicant pursues the company, not the other way around. But getting an informational interview with the Human Resources department was a challenge. I was a nobody at a no-name magazine, living in an irrelevant city for publishing.

I was determined to get an informational interview.

I emailed everyone I knew. Everyone I'd met through *LA Livin'* or from press events. I was manic about it. Finally, after weeks of radio silence I heard back from someone.

I took a deep breath before reading the email. "Janet Martinez passed along your information and I would be happy to meet with you on an exploratory basis. Please let me know the next time that you will be in New York," signed Sarah Lee Porter, the Director of Human Resources/Editorial of Condé Nast, at 4 Times Square, New York, New York.

I re-read the email. And then I read it four more times after that. *Lucky* magazine had been my favorite magazine for years, and its parent company, Condé Nast, was one of the most impossible-to-get-into publishing houses in the country, if not the most. Someone from Condé had just emailed me. On purpose. *How was this happening?*

I wrote Sarah Lee Porter back immediately and lied, saying I'd be in New York in a week. Once she confirmed our interview I booked a round-trip ticket and called up my friend Kymm. She traveled frequently and loved New York—I had a hunch a visit to Manhattan would be of interest to her.

~~~~~~

Unlike every guy in Hollywood, Ben was unexpectedly tall, around six feet five inches, and handsome in a way that was equally as unfamiliar to me, with a lazily shaven face and deep, brooding eyes. His whole vibe reminded me of a lumberjack. Like he'd spent his life cutting down trees or tossing a tree trunk over his shoulder.

Kymm and I were in New York for my upcoming informational interview, and she asked me to come with her to a sports bar to watch an Ohio State basketball game. Having spent so much time surrounded by the "models and bottles" *LA Livin'* nightclub scene, where horny rich men spend upwards of $3,000 a night to order Costco-sized bottles of Belvedere vodka to their table so that rail thin models will sit with them, I was refreshed at the thought of going to a bar where drinks were less than 10 dollars and there was nowhere to sit.

Kymm and I were walking through the sticky dance floor when I felt someone pinch my elbow. It was a soft pinch. More like a squeeze. The squeeze was connected to a hand and the hand was connected to an arm. I traced the arm up to the shoulder and then up another foot, where I met the soulful eyes of a tall, dark, and handsome stranger.

"Can I get you a drink?" the elbow-pincher said rather flirtatiously, leaning over my shoulder to talk. His name was Ben. He wore a black button-down shirt with the top button undone. I got the feeling that he always left that button open.

"Hi," I said coyly. I looked at what he was drinking. "Um, I'll have a Bud Light, too," I said, immediately regretting my decision because I detested the taste of beer. Fortunately for me, elbow-pinching Tall Ben proved to be astute and noticed that, after handing me a Bud Light, I didn't take one sip.

"Do you want something else?"

"Yeah, do you mind if I get a vodka soda?"

"Not at all. Here, give me that," he said, taking the beer out of my hand. Then he gave the bartender a quick nod and ordered me a new cocktail.

We leaned against the dark mahogany bar and were transfixed with one another for the rest of the night, talking, laughing, and eventually exchanging phone numbers and a kiss before I left. I had an interview the next day for a potential job in New York City and I wanted to get a good night's sleep, so there was nothing that was going to keep me out. Not even Tall Ben with the top button unbuttoned shirt.

The Condé Nast building was enormous, with long sheets of glass angled high above the entryway, and a check-in desk that had five people working at it, all wearing perfectly pressed suits. I told one of the security guards my name and who I was there to see, and she made a phone call to verify. I thought about Matt and Sammy and Annalise back at *LA Livin'*, and how their lack of credentials would deny them a meeting inside of Condé Nast. I was a real aspiring editor. They could fool Hollywood as much as they wanted, but they could never get passed the dapper security desk at 4 Times Square.

"Here you are," said the security officer as she handed me a visitor's pass with my name on it and pointed to a bank of elevators behind her. "Take one from the far end." Only certain elevators went to certain floors.

I stepped inside the correct elevator, and rather than seeing floor numbers I saw the names of magazines. I scanned them indulgently as the elevator flew me up to my meeting.

GQ. Allure. And then, there it was. My fashion bible. *Lucky.*

Ping. The doors opened three floors later and I quickly peeled the backing off of my nametag and placed it onto the soft lapel of my Theory blazer.

Sarah Lee met me at the elevator bank. "Thanks for coming in," she said, extending her hand out to shake mine.

I followed her into her office.

She gazed at my bag and saw a large leather portfolio sticking out of it. "Is that your portfolio? May I see it?"

"Oh, yes." I handed it to her with a huge smile. I'd spent days putting it together. Each article had its own plastic sheet protector, and it was organized by topics: fashion, beauty, fitness, food, and photo shoots that I'd directed.

I watched as she flipped each page. "I'm happy you emailed, but I have to be honest, I've never heard of *LA Livin'* magazine."

No one had. "I understand, we are based in Los Angeles" — she interrupted me.

"I'm impressed with the amount of work here. And I recognize the names of many of these photographers."

I pinched my thigh. Some of them were big name photographers, and I knew that, but I didn't actually believe it until I was 3,000 miles away from my home base and heard a valid Human Resources professional say so.

"Most entry-level editors spend their time fact-checking," she said, still thumbing through my work. "This is really phenomenal stuff—you've worked with photographers that have shot for some of our magazines. And wow, you produced a cover shoot with Paris Hilton."

She swiveled her chair away from me to read something written down on a notepad, then she swiveled back. Her chair made a slight squeal. "There is an Assistant Editor opening at *Cooking* magazine that you'd be perfect for," she said. "Can I hold onto your book? I think the editors should see it."

My brain lost all function and went blank. I felt as though I'd just been given the Nobel Prize in Literature. Sarah Lee thought I, the girl who used to get cars detailed for her boss and cry during lunch breaks, could work with real editors in New York?

"Yes, definitely hold onto it. That sounds very exciting."

"Great. Well I have another meeting in a few minutes, why don't I walk you out?"

I held my composure until I got to the lobby then speed-walked through the atrium until I was outside. I perched on a ledge, unfastened my heels so that I could change into walking flats, and called Mom.

"They said I'd be great for a cooking magazine, can you believe it?" I blurted when she answered.

Mom was ecstatic, screaming for Dad to come close so he could hear. "Jack, Jaaaaack," she giggled into the receiver.

While she certainly didn't like the idea of me moving

across the country, she'd always been my number one career supporter. She knew how unhappy I was at *LA Livin'* and how much I respected real publishing houses.

"Beki's interview went great, Jack. This is the biggest magazine publisher in the country and they want to hire her," she screamed. I could hear her smiling through each word.

"Mom, mom," I shouted. "No one hired me, but they like me." She always embellished my achievements.

An interview meant a job offer; a job offer meant I would be President.

But, because the world is a cruel place, as soon as I hung up with Mom I got a work email from Mary on my BlackBerry.

The subject line read: You will not believe this.

I scrolled down and learned that Sofia, the smoking hot secretary from Peru who'd let several of the guys from the office do lines off her boobs at a party recently, had just been promoted from her post as office secretary to Director of Events. It also came with a raise.

I'd been with the company for two years, and even though I had a title change, Matt wouldn't give me a raise. He and HR came up with asinine reasons to avoid paying me more or giving me an annual review. The thought of Sofia getting a pay increase and extremely unfair promotion made me boil. She was ruining it for the rest of us. *That stupid fucking bitch*, I wanted to scream into the air.

I started to write Mary back: "I'm not surprised," I started.

Then I made myself stop.

Something inside of me—perhaps the voice of reason—told me not to even respond to Mary.

I looked out into the sea of fast-moving Midtown working people and took a deep breath in through my nose like I'd been taught many times to do in therapy. I held my breath for exactly seven seconds, then exhaled slowly out of my mouth for eight counts. The air was filthy and warm, and it brought me instant joy. I repeated my breathing sequence three more times until I regained control. I had one more night in New York so I chose to ignore the office politics and focus on the promising interview. *Do not even engage with anyone at work right now*, I reminded myself. It was the learning experience Dad wanted me to have. I needed to learn how to not react.

That night I was invited to the opening of a brand new club in the trendy Meatpacking District. I'd never even heard of the Meatpacking District, but I had a hunch the party would be good because Mary connected me with a publicist friend of hers from Alison Brod Public Relations that was helping to host the event. I made the first move and texted Tall Ben.

"Hey you," I wrote on my BlackBerry. I was disappointed after the great conversation and kiss we'd shared the night earlier that he hadn't reached out to me first.

"Was just going to text you," he responded, so obviously

lying. But I didn't care. I was emboldened by being in New York and felt myself differently.

"If you don't have plans you should come meet me at Tenjune in the Meatpacking." In the Meatpacking? Was that even grammatically correct? Should I have just written "in Meatpacking?" I gave him the details and said I'd be there around 11:00 p.m.

At midnight Tall Ben showed up to Tenjune in the Meatpacking and sent me a text message saying that he was outside. The party was packed, and the line outside of the club was as thick as the summer air, with girls in mini dresses pushing their thighs into the velvet rope to prove their hotness to an army of burly bouncers. I didn't have the social clout to get Tall Ben through the club's gatekeepers on my own so I found a guy named Eugene that was running the show.

"That guy in the white button-up is my cousin," I said, pointing at Tall Ben who was doing his best not to look embarrassed that he couldn't get in. "He's supposed to be in here with me. We got separated."

Then I name-dropped the publicist that initially invited me. "You work with Alison Brod PR, right?" I asked, already knowing the answer.

With a quick flick of the wrist, Eugene waved Tall Ben through a moshpit of jealous people. For that moment, I saw the value of someone like Peter from *LA Livin'*: the guy that could get anyone into a party.

"Thanks," Tall Ben said, coming in to kiss me.

I used my hip to push him aside, noticing that his top button was undone. "I told the guy you were my cousin," I said, smiling.

He smirked, relieved that I wasn't rejecting him and we headed for the subterranean club.

When the night ended we went our separate ways: I to my hotel, he to his apartment in the Financial District. I knew better than to sleep with him right away—that rule had always steered my moral compass—but I was into him.

I knew I'd be seeing him again.

Somehow.

On Monday I returned to *LA Livin'* feeling on top of the world. I'd met a really nice, really bright guy, went to a club opening, and even had a great meeting at Condé Nast. Mary and I both got into the office early, and she eagerly asked me for an update on the interview.

"The Condé Nast building is magical, Mary. I felt like a princess, like a journalist princess," I shared.

"I know, it's the best."

I forgot she used to work there when she was the Editor at *YM* magazine.

"This HR rep said there might be a junior-level editor opening at *Cooking* magazine, which is kind of funny because I don't know anything about cooking. But it would be a starting point and I'd have fun talking to my mom about new recipes."

Mary crinkled her forehead.

"Maybe I'd get to work on lifestyle stories at some point," I finished.

"Condé Nast doesn't own *Cooking* magazine," she said quickly. "I think you mean *Cookie*, the mothering magazine."

"Oh, are you sure?" I asked, feeling stupid. How could I make such a mistake? If I didn't even know what magazines Condé Nast published, how could I ever work for them?

"Rebecca," she said holding back a smile. "It's a magazine about parenting, you know you can't authentically write about that."

"Shit."

~~~~~~~~~~

Nothing much ever came of my meeting with Sarah Lee. I sent numerous follow-up emails, and she responded to only one. She then put me in touch with someone named Kristen who handled junior-level editorial openings, which meant that Kristen became my new target. From there, Kristen sent me a job opening at *Condé Nast Traveler*. And from there, an editor sent me a 22-page edit test to complete.

Nothing came of that either.

From there I flew out to New York again, that time for an informational interview at Time Inc., and then I flew out a third time for a meeting at Hearst Magazines, but with the Executive Editor of *CosmoGIRL*. Every meeting and email brought me one step closer to my ultimate goal of landing an editorial job in New York, just not close enough.

I couldn't wait anymore. I had to go, even without an offer.

The idea of moving away from home terrified me, but I'd learned through therapy that I should welcome the sensation of fear. Running from fear created a cyclical sensation in which I'd become more afraid of being afraid than of the thing itself. I was more scared to be scared than I was scared to actually move. In other words I needed to just move to New York, scared and all.

It was 11:00 a.m. on a workday when I opened up a new tab in my Firefox browser and typed in a flight search. It had been many months since my first professional visit to New York and I couldn't sit still any longer in California.

One-way. Los Angeles International Airport to John F. Kennedy.

"Mary, I'm doing it. I'm buying this ticket." I smiled, waiting for the screen to load.

She stopped typing and looked up at me, grinning demurely. "I'll never find another writer like you, but you don't belong at this crazy place. You need to go to New York."

She wasn't the first person to tell me this. All my life, cousins and casual acquaintances made remarks that suggested I didn't belong in L.A. I didn't really know what that meant, but they always said it as if it was a compliment. Mary got out of her seat and came over to hug me. The hug said so much.

She was going to stay and suffer alone in order to save me.

I quietly walked through the office and onto Sunset Boulevard so that I could call Ben. He was no longer just Tall Ben; he was my Ben. We'd continued to date since the weekend we met, flying back and forth across the country every month or so, and I knew he'd be happy to hear the news. He wasn't the reason I was moving, though. If I thought about our relationship in publishing terms, I wanted to make a deal with New York. Ben was just added value.

He worked as a software developer in a quiet office in Midtown. I never called him during the day, so he knew something was up when his phone rang.

"Hey, what's going on?" he whispered.

"I know you're working, but I did it. I quit," I said.

"Wait, what? You quit?" His voice grew louder.

Moving without a job wasn't something he or I thought would ever happen, but it was my new reality. If I wanted to escape *LA Livin'*, Mom, and everything else, I'd have to be the bravest person I knew and relocate without a job.

"I QUIT! And I already bought a one-way ticket out. Twelve days from now. I'm getting out of this place." I couldn't actually believe the words I was saying.

Over the two and a half years I'd worked at *LA Livin'*, I'd managed to save $8,342, even with all of my cross-country flying. If I could find a room to rent in New York City for under $800 a month, that meant I could last, at the very least, six months without a job. I hadn't actually figured out my cost of living—therapy certainly wasn't cheap—but six months at $800 seemed reasonable.

"I'm so fucking proud of you," Ben said. He knew everything that was going on and that the company I worked for was toxic.

We'd been dating long-distance for many months and were exclusive, but Ben loved the three-day weekend version of me. When he flew to see me in L.A. he came to a clean apartment that I shared with a girlfriend. I had a fully stocked fridge. My hair was done and my underwear always matched. We'd drive up the coast to Malibu for lunch, and end the night at exclusive launch parties at the Playboy Mansion or at sprawling homes in the Hollywood Hills where we'd leave with fistfuls of swag and specialty candy. In New York, he'd take me to dinners and the theater, and I'd put on my best face.

He had no idea that "Rebecca LA The Hottie" (that's how he saved my name in his phone the night we met) was actually a "slightly-to-moderately panic-ridden girl with a suppressed yet debilitating fear of being dead and an inability to leave home."

He didn't know that I'd never successfully lived more

than 100 miles away from Mom before.

He didn't know she was my black hole.

I told Ben that I'd call him later that night because I needed to call my parents and tell them the good news. Spending even just 45 seconds on the phone with Ben, knowing that Mom was at home completely in the dark, sent fireworks of angst popping off inside of me.

Mom answered the phone on one ring like she always did. "I did it, Mom. I quit and I bought a ticket, I am moving to New York."

I wanted to hear joy in her voice the way I'd heard it when I called her after my Condé Nast interview, but I could only hear the sounds of the TV in the background. She must have been in the kitchen. "Mom, did you hear me? I'm moving to New York!"

There was a long pause. More TV.

"That's great, honey." Her voice was monotone, as if I were calling her to tell her that blueberries were on sale at Ralph's supermarket.

"Mom, you sound upset. I need you to be happy for me."

"Sweetie, I have something boiling on the stove, I really need to take it off before it burns."

My heart fell. Her response was cold. I needed her more than ever, and she knew that. I'd never be strong enough to welcome the fearful unknown of moving away from her without her help. She knew that too. "Mom, don't do this," I wailed into the phone.

"I'm very happy for you. I have to go." Then she hung up.

I wasn't surprised. I frantically dialed back.

It rang four times and then the answering machine picked up. I called again and that time I got Dad. Mom had already filled him in and he tried to calm me down.

"You know your mother. She's sad to see you leave but we are so happy for you. Just give her a minute to process this."

He did his best, but it fell short. I needed Mom's sign-off to feel like I'd made the right choice. I needed it immediately.

I left work early and went home to my apartment to start packing up my life. My BlackBerry vibrated. I had an email. It was from Ben.

The subject line was: Reasons Ben might not be good for Rebecca.

The email contained a list of his self-proclaimed faults, just to make sure I knew what I was getting into. Aside from being drop dead handsome and incredibly bright, he was refreshingly funny. A mash-up of self-deprecating humor and youthful satire. No one in Los Angeles was ever self-deprecating. I'd never met a hot guy in Los Angeles who wanted to make me laugh.

Ben and I were about to get the unedited round-the-clock version of each other and even after reading his list

I was worried he'd be disappointed to learn who I really was. Had I shared *enough* with him?

His email list of "cons" included things like "I'm a terrible cook and I eat quesadillas constantly" and "I sweat profusely from June to September." The second one explained the unbuttoned top button—he needed the extra breathing room. These things were a hiccup compared to my flaws. He knew I left Michigan because I didn't want to be there, but he didn't know the real story behind how it unfolded. He had no idea that I'd never successfully lived farther than a 100-mile radius of home and that I'd probably never even really make it to New York, and if I did, I'd find a way to send myself down a dark path, or perhaps even get kicked out. How would I even respond to his email?

Maybe I'd write him a book.

I was 26 years old by the time I landed in New York, ready to become a resident of the great state and city. Since Ben and I weren't ready to live together, he found me a sublet in the Financial District, just a few blocks away from his apartment.

I'd packed up dozens of boxes and sent them to Ben's apartment via UPS Ground because he lived in a doorman building and that was the only sure way to guarantee that, no matter what time UPS delivered the packages, someone would be there to sign for them. Otherwise, the future of my boxed belongings would be grim. If the UPS delivery driver decided to leave the packages on Ben's doorstep they'd probably get stolen, and if the driver sent them back to the sorting warehouse, I'd probably be forced to trek somewhere ridiculously far like Roosevelt Island. I didn't know much about life in Manhattan, but I knew about optimizing for deliveries.

Leaving Los Angeles was painful, especially for Mom, who had an impossible time joining Dad in the car to drop me off at the airport. She stuffed a few "Lucky Bucks" in my hand when we got into the car at home, but couldn't get out to hug me once we arrived at the airport. She was sobbing and didn't want me to see. She wanted me to go so badly.

"I'm sorry, I just can't watch you leave. I'm too weak," she said to me while fighting tears.

I nodded.

Weeks of non-stop nausea and unrest made me numb to her emotional outpouring.

We were quite a pair.

In the days leading up to my departure, I sat on the phone with Ben crying. I needed Mom to support my decision to move, otherwise I didn't have faith that I could do it. He listened silently, unable to solve the problem, which, as a software developer, drove him mad. Ben thrived on cracking puzzles, but my relationship with Mom was proving to be an impossible brain teaser. There was no solution: I had to accept that I was doing this thing alone.

When Mom and Dad dropped me off at the airport I knew I had the confidence to board the plane, but I was more robot than girl. A shell of a person following an itinerary.

Walk here, you. Turn right, human. Sit plane. Buckle up.

Ben was leaning against the wall at baggage claim when I arrived at JFK seven hours later, holding a raspberry yogurt and a mint-flavored Balance Bar, both for me. I ran to him for an immediate emotional resuscitation and buried my head in the softness of his down parka.

Attempted Robbery, 2008

Everyone that lives in New York has a "my first brush with crime" story. Your friend will probably come late to a dinner party and apologize for her tardiness by saying, "Sorry, there was a crazy woman outside of my apartment screaming at everyone that she had a gun so I had to wait until she left before I went outside, but here, I brought some jelly I made." Everyone will ask about her preserving techniques because "crazy lady screaming nonsense" no longer warrants worry from friends. People just don't care to hear about it anymore.

Except me.

I live for these terrifying stories partly because I can't believe people survive them. Someone had a gun and you lived? That's not technically possible. According to everything I learned from Mom there is no plausible way to survive a Woman With Pistol on a city block.

Tell me everything. Wait, let me get a pen.

~~~~~~~~~

Mariel was a fun girl who worked in fashion and lived in her own apartment in the East Village, in a doorman building with golden hardwood floors. I'd known her from home—we went to elementary school together for a short period of time, so she wasn't technically a new friend—but I pulled a lot of pranks on her when we were kids so I was surprised and excited when she wanted to hang out with me in New York. Once in fifth grade I pulled her shorts down in front of the whole class. It seemed funny at the time.

Two months into my Manhattan residency I'd only learned how to use the A/C/E train line so that limited where I felt comfortable going without Ben. The seemingly nonsensical range of numbers and colors made my head spin, so to feel in control I stuck to the line I knew.

One night Mariel asked me to meet her for dinner in SoHo and since I knew how to get to SoHo, I said yes. I still didn't have a job, so I rarely did anything extravagant, like going out to dinner. I wasn't punishing myself. I just needed to make sure that my $8,342 lasted as long as it could. But I needed to get out of my apartment and out of the cyclical job hunt—I was married to my computer, refreshing my inbox constantly in hopes that a magazine wanted to bring me in for an interview.

It was early evening on one of those transitional weather days when you can feel that the winter bite is over and spring is nearby. "It's breaking," Ben's roommate Roman would say, referring to the temperature. Weather breaking in New York was practically a legal holiday.

Since it was almost spring, I decided to wear a dress. I put on a tight blue jersey knit number and brown ankle boots to honor the change in temperature, despite being told never to wear dresses at night on the subway. When I moved to New York everyone sent me off with a bunch of rules, the most popular of which was "Never stop walking in the middle of the street."

The second nugget of wisdom related to above-the-knee apparel. I ignored the advice and thought that if I wore the dress with heavy boots that would offset the sexiness that the dress evoked. It made sense at the time.

At Canal Street, the train came to its routine stop and the train operator's voice came over the speakers. I was still fairly new to New York so I listened to every single announcement like my life depended on it.

There was a loud buzz, then a crackle sound, like it was the first time the train radio had been turned on. "Ladies and gentlemen, there is an unruly passenger on the train with a knife. Please kindly exit the train and"—I jumped out of my seat before the announcement ended. Everyone did. Even those wearing headphones. And we pushed our way onto the platform and into the next train across the platform, but the doors wouldn't shut. They just sat open, leaving us exposed to the danger we'd just run away from.

I didn't know what to do so I stood in the doorway of my subway car. I thought that at least I'd get a better view if Knife Guy left my original train and got onto the new one, and I'd be in a great position if I needed to run off. As an additional layer of defense, I opened my legs out wide like I'd been taught to do in high school basketball practice when rebounding the ball. It was called boxing out. I needed a sturdy foundation in case someone came running toward me.

I should've worn flats.

I began to pant heavily, listening to my echoing heartbeat, and wondering if I would die on the subway, just two months into my time as a New Yorker. In this blue dress. I was minutes into imagining myself getting stabbed by the elusive Knife Guy when the subway beeped and the doors closed, which I took to mean that either Knife Guy was apprehended or he stayed on the express line. I backed away from the door and held onto a pole in my train car to catch my breath and process the danger that I'd just escaped.

And because the world is always a cruel place, someone started harassing me almost immediately.

"Whoo, whoo," echoed from the other end of the car. A man was whistling. They were airy whistles. I stupidly looked at him.

He was wearing old jeans and sitting in a way that took

up more space than he deserved. "Look at those lovely legs, girl," he catcalled at me, inching his knees further out to the side.

Gross.

I swiveled on my heel and turned my back toward him, yanking my dress down toward my knees as far as it would go, even if it meant exposing more of my chest than I would've liked. He continued calling for me, letting out "Yahhh" groans from his end of the car on and off like a metronome. My legs felt chilly and prickly. *Why was no one telling this vile man to stop howling at me? We all just narrowly escaped death*, I thought. *Shouldn't we be a tight-knit group now?*

At Spring Street the doors opened and I sprinted off the train and up the stairs, taking two steps at a time.

Mariel was already seated outdoors at a lovely Italian restaurant when I ran up and plopped down in the seat across from her, knocking the wooden chair on two legs before steadying myself.

"You'll never believe what happened," I told her. Then I went on to tell her all about the Knife Guy and the Yahhh Guy, and how scared I was and how nobody was going to help me, but when the waiter walked over she politely put her palm in my face and motioned for me to stop talking.

I thought she was going to tell him that we needed a minute. Maybe Mariel wanted me to call my mom to let her know that I'd somehow survived the scariest encounter of all the scary encounters. Heck, maybe Mariel would want to call her mom, too.

She glanced down at her menu, then back at me. "Sorry, I'm starving, do you know what you want to eat?"

I laughed through my nose, then ordered.

～～～～～～

Every nighttime conversation with Mom involved the same queries. She needed to know where, exactly, I was. Tenth Avenue? First Avenue? Then she'd ask, "Are there people around you?" and I'd mutter, "Yes, this is New York there are always people around," and then she'd say, "Beki, don't be smart. It's a moment like this when you're not focused and you're carelessly walking and talking on the phone that something could happen. Are there a lot of people out?"

People around meant you would be safe.

People around meant that no one could get you.

One night, I took an empty seat toward the rear of a reasonably crowded Number 16 bus in the Upper East Side. I was headed home to Ben's and my apartment—we'd recently moved in together. I sent Mom a quick text.

"Sorry didn't call. Chased the bus. Just got on, will call you when I get home." It wasn't our preferred method of communication, but I thought a text would suffice and ward off the bad juju that surely would've come if I hadn't reached out at all.

About 20 blocks south someone standing behind me in

the exit well leaned over my shoulder and grabbed hold of my wrist.

Squeeze.

I turned around slowly—smiling, even—expecting to recognize the person.

But I didn't.

Hundreds of needles pricked the back of my neck. There in front of me was a stranger in a maroon sweatshirt standing in the exit doorway, grabbing for my cell phone.

I knew better than to sit directly in front of the back exit door. Mom taught me about public transportation safety when I was a child. "Stand before you ever sit down in that row," Mom would say. "You're just asking to get robbed; you're easy pickings and they have a quick getaway."

The guy yanked my arm hard, forcing me to swivel my body weight in his direction. I dug the pads of my fingertips into my phone and yanked it back in my direction, pulling his body weight and maroon sweatshirt toward me.

He pulled even harder.

Everything I had learned about being mugged suggested that engaging in a tug-of-war contest was the poorest option. Shouting crazy things to scare this man off or just letting go of the device altogether would have been by-the-book mother-approved moves, but I disregarded what I knew Mom would have wanted me to do, and instead found the strength to do what I wanted to do. I pulled back, harnessing all the power I had.

Holy shit, I pulled him really hard. His elbow slammed into the metal frame of my seat.

"Fuuuuuuck," my bus bandit shouted.

He let go of my arm and darted out the back door as soon as the bus pulled over for its regular stop.

I could feel my pulse vibrating through my body. I bent down to collect my things so I could escape the sensation and get off the bus.

"No, don't go out there. He's just standing there waiting and he's holding something," an older woman sitting directly across from me said. She had grocery packages sitting on her lap. Trader Joe's.

I looked out of the window and saw my attempted robber standing against a brick wall. My pulse became a full-blown speaker system, playing fear on repeat.

I hunched over, faced the aisle in case someone else wanted to screw with me, and stared at my fingers as they hurriedly tried to connect with the correct numbers on my key pad. It was no use. The pain in my chest was insurmountable. Ignoring it would only fuel it. I had to own the fact that I was having a panic attack.

"Some … someone … someone," I said, trembling, once I finally dialed Ben. My voice was inaudible, but I managed to get the crucial facts across. "Come to the 23rd Street stop," I said and hung up, zipping my phone into my bag.

I spent the next 30 blocks wondering why I even moved to New York. What was I even doing there? I fell into an existential headspin.

Why had I moved to New York?

I wanted to become a revered magazine editor and had grossly naïve dreams of rubbing shoulders with powerful players like *Vanity Fair's* Graydon Carter. The same way people moved to Manhattan to become the next Carrie Bradshaw, except I just wanted her career. I had no interest in clomping around Midtown in snakeskin Jimmy Choos or going to brunch with my best friends. I hated brunch. It made no sense.

All I wanted was for city dwellers to pick up their favorite magazine every month and see something I wrote in it: How to [trim/slim/elim] your [something] in just 5 steps! By Rebecca Brown. Applause would follow. And maybe a book deal, but if I took too long to write it, then I'd settle for self-publishing...

Instead, I was taking public transportation down 2nd Avenue and rubbing up against the seedy underbelly of New York City. I was a fool to think I'd be able to avoid it that long. I was on the bus, after all. The only things more dangerous than traveling on a bus were walking around alone in the evening on a street full of pedophilic Santas, or parking by a dented van at the mall. Lessons Mom had learned from Grandpa. Lessons I had been taught at her knee.

The bus took its sweet time pulling over on 23rd Street. The brakes squealed as it came to its stop and I jumped out with so much force you would have thought someone threw me off. Ben was standing in front of our neighborhood deli, Bruno Ravioli. A flickering light in the sausage display window illuminated his silhouette and I ran to him.

"What the heck happened, I didn't understand a word you said." I belted out a loud cough, then a single whimper that lasted for five seconds. I wiped my nose on the sleeve of his gray hooded Duke sweatshirt. My anxiety began to abate as I filled him in.

"Nothing is going to happen to you," he said, firmly.

Ben put my bags on his shoulder and held me tightly as we walked home together. Before he put the key into the door I tugged at his sweatshirt sleeve.

"Don't tell my mom. She'll think this happened because I didn't call her."

I couldn't tell her. This was the moment she had been preparing me for, after all.

I'd finally unmoored myself from Mom and learned how to forge my own identity. I'd packed up my anxiety disorder and gone to New York to figure out how to panic on my own; it was a huge risk. If I told her that the anonymous threat she said would be waiting for me when I left her in California had finally materialized while living in New York, I'd have lost everything I fought so hard to find.

Everything I fought so hard to be.

I didn't care if she was right or wrong, I just didn't want

to give her the satisfaction that someone had finally found me with my guard down and robbed me.

I sat on that thought as we walked into the apartment, then paused in the doorway.

Wait, I exhaled. *Maroon sweatshirt fuckface hadn't robbed me.*

Maroon sweatshirt fuckface found me in the worst seat imaginable on the bus that Mom told me to never sit in, and he made every attempt to rob me, but he actually didn't rob me.

He only *tried* to rob me.

I stood up tall in the living room. Now I wanted to call Mom and shout the story right into her ear. Every detail of it. Maroon sweatshirt fuckface tried to rob me, Mom.

But I. Fucking. Won.

Fishhooked on the 6, 2010

The fierce blast of air conditioner that usually smacked my face when the subway car doors opened didn't hit me like it was supposed to. I cautiously stepped inside the steamy north-bound 6 train and looked around. Bubbles of condensation collected on the windows. This was not a good sign. *Fuck, the air is broken again,* I sighed. It was a rainy June morning around 7:30 a.m. and I was on the subway headed uptown.

I pushed through the crowded car and grabbed onto the subway pole with my left hand. The doors closed. It was even more humid than I thought. Buried deep at the other end of the car a man was asking for money. I slyly peeled my left hand off the pole just long enough to dig into the deep pocket of my khaki London Fog raincoat, find my iPhone, and turn up the volume.

If I couldn't hear him, I couldn't help him. The New York motto.

I'd just been hired at newly launched *Manhattan* magazine

as an Associate Editor and could barely contain my excitement each morning as I left my apartment. I'd never been a smiler—someone that just smiled for no reason—but heading uptown toward Rockefeller Center for work branded my face with a much-needed smile. My Senior Editor came from *Lucky*; my Managing Editor came from *Maxim*; and my Editor-in-Chief came from *Complex*. These were real vetted editors—the people Mary told me worked in New York—and I was working with them. Me. Someone from a no-name magazine whose previous coworkers were lauded for their party know-how.

Every survived moment as a resident of Manhattan bolstered my self-confidence. I did it; I left Los Angeles. I never wanted to go back there. I was weak when I lived there and I knew it. Decisions in Los Angeles needed to be approved by Mom, or in the very least, talked through with her. In New York, I'd learned to make decisions and tell her about them later. In New York I was brave; in New York I could ride the subway.

Out of my peripheral vision I could see the panhandler begin to nudge his way through the crowded car, forcing riders into contortionist poses so he could pass.

The train made a loud belch.

Ah, the air conditioner kicked on, I thought, grinning.

I hated interacting with people on the train, so I quickly glanced in the panhandler's direction to size up the situation. Having experienced an attempted robbery on the bus, I was always on high alert, even when it was something as common as someone asking for money.

I saw what looked like a scruffy young guy in black sunglasses carrying an umbrella. He shuffled through the crowd slowly, heading my way.

I looked away to avoid eye contact.

Seconds later, the guy walked toward me with his right hand extended out firmly like a fire poker. I turned my head in his direction to see why he was pointing at me, and felt something rough slide into my mouth and scratch against the inside of my cheek.

"Aggh," I howled, jumping back in horror and forcing people to catch me as I demanded their floorspace.

I fixated on the back of the man's head as he passed me, looking for an explanation, when the gears clicked: Sunglass-sporting-man-with-umbrella was really blind-homeless-man-with-walking-stick and his fingers had accidentally just gone into my mouth.

There was nowhere to go. Every turn of the head left me staring at a swath of passengers, none of whom had the decency to ask me if I was okay. I left my mouth propped open, half in horror and half hoping that whatever bacteria were now brewing inside of my mouth would be killed by the powerful subway air-conditioning, which was now on full blast. Or that maybe someone would feel bad for me and offer to squirt hand sanitizer onto my tongue. I would've accepted it gratefully.

I rushed off the train at 51st Street and ran to my office, my purse, hair, and tongue all flying around wildly. I pushed open the door of the ladies room and bent over the sink so that I could spit myself to safety. Then, as I'd done in middle school the first time I tried marijuana, I shoved a dollop of soap into my mouth. I was thankful for the bitter taste. It's how I knew it was working.

Gargle, spit.

Gargle, spit.

In my office, I called Mom.

"I am probably going to die," I told her. "This would never happen in California. I'm Googling hand-to-mouth infections now," I continued, furiously typing away on my computer with my left hand as I held the phone with my right. I stared at the glass office door hoping no one would come in. "Do you think I should get bleach? A tetanus shot?"

I rifled through a stack of papers on my desk, and furiously clicked the top of my retractable pen. I thought Mom would console me and tell me to come home right away. I thought she'd say she was disappointed that I wasn't more aware of my surroundings.

But Mom didn't say any of those things. Instead, she just laughed a long, loud cackle, as though either the story—or the absurdity of it—was familiar to her.

"Are you out of your mind? You'll end up killing yourself with bleach," she yelled, still piercing my ear with laughter. Barely able to catch her breath, she added, "Boy, are you my daughter."

"So no bleach?" I asked, flinging the pen toward the pen holster on my desk.

"I have to tell your father this story."

Fishhooking, as it seemed, would be the crisis that healthily separated us. It would be the near-death event in which Mom stopped guiding me, and instead, viewed me as capable. I no longer needed her to survive.

I could just, well, survive.

Even if it meant a homeless man's fingers might accidentally slide into my mouth from time to time, it was a fair price to pay.

Part III

Stuck in New York, 2012

"Well, I'm crushed you're not coming with me, but I will say one thing: I am not going to miss you asking me to place a fresh water glass on the window sill every week," Ben said trying desperately to make us laugh.

I continued the Germano family tradition I inherited from Grandpa Charlie. Charlie Germano was a tall and loud man who cut hair for a living. He owned a barber shop on the main drag in Southampton, New York, and there wasn't a local in town that didn't know him. Anyone who wanted that old-world Italian charm and a stellar haircut went to see him at Job's Lane Tonsorial, and old timers that just wanted to talk about how they did that day betting on the ponies at the OTB would spend an afternoon sitting at his shop. The place reeked of cigar smoke—one of his bad habits.

Mom and I spent every summer before I went to France at my grandparents' house at 26 Argonne Road in Hampton Bays. It was a modest two-bedroom house, with one air-conditioning unit in the spare bedroom. Grandpa would've rather sweat all through the August night than put something in his window that could easily be opened. They might get Grandma, who sometimes slept in the spare room with the air conditioner, but they weren't going to get him, he'd say. Every night before he went to bed, he'd wedge a dining chair underneath the front and back door knobs, and place glasses of water on his window sill. That way the doors could never be forced open, and if someone did manage to crack a window, the glass would fall and crash, waking him up and hopefully scaring the bad guys off. I never understood why the glasses needed water, but there was an Italian science to it I'm sure.

According to Mom, at some point in my grandfather's 40s, while he was working as a barber and moonlighting as a bookie to the Mafia in Hell's Kitchen, he borrowed way more money than he could pay back. So late one night, he packed up Mom, her sister Suzanne, and Grandma and told them it was time to leave their apartment in Brooklyn. It had worn out its welcome. He drove them out to Long Island, where no one would think to look for him.

Most of the stories I know about my grandfather came via my mother—by the time I was old enough to develop a relationship with Grandpa he was without a voice. Throat cancer. But even a laryngectomy at 80 wasn't going to stop an old Italian guy from talking. After he beat cancer he left

Hampton Bays and came to live with us in Santa Monica. I was still in high school at the time, but I was entranced by him.

At six feet two inches tall, he was nearly all upper-body, with arms so disproportionately long they were almost alien looking. When Grandpa spoke his hands danced. He flicked his wrists and used all of his fingers for emphasis. I stared at him wide-eyed when he told stories. They always ended in a punchline of some sort. And whatever he couldn't tell me by whispering with his raspy voice he'd write down in all caps on scratch pieces of paper.

One time he and I walked to the upscale Brentwood Country Mart a few blocks away from my parents' house for lunch, and a couple carrying matching tennis rackets asked if they could sit down with us and share the table. Grandpa nodded silently and waved his hand at them like they were royalty, then pulled a small notepad out of his shirt pocket and wrote me a note in his blocky handwriting.

"STINKING YUPPIES."

I had a hard time understanding that relocating merely 90 miles away from Brooklyn to Hampton Bays would hide my grandfather from what Mom says would have been a gory death by Mafiosi, but he lived to be 92 and no one ever got him. Perhaps all his precautions worked. I never picked up the chair routine because it was far more challenging to find chairs that would angle perfectly underneath a door knob, but the window trick was easy enough to copy. It got exhausting because you had to remember to move the glass when you wanted to open the window, which is why I was always asking Ben to replace it before we went to bed. I'd be sound asleep, hear him come into the bedroom, remember that the water glass was moved, and ask him to please put it back. Because if you remembered that the glass was missing and didn't replace it, that would be the night you got robbed. It was a chore but Ben did it. He was a keeper.

"I'm sure your mom can give you another tactic to use instead of the water glass," he said jokingly, again, forcing humor into the room.

For three years Ben and I lived together in a ground floor Manhattan apartment on East 22nd Street. We filled the unit with love, mostly, along with some hand-me-down furniture I procured from my generous cousin April who also lived out in the Hamptons, and ugly things from Ben's college years that I couldn't, no matter how hard I tried, convince him to get rid of.

"This practically has bugs living inside it," I'd say about his filthy navy blue Nautica comforter, before giving in to the fight and neatly placing it at the foot of our bed.

Ben was moving out of our apartment, and it was our last day together in our mostly lovely home. He was following his dream of making the world better by joining a nonprofit educational tech startup in Silicon Valley, California. He was a computer programmer—a career I knew zero things about when we first started dating—and while he loved me and his job and our home in New York, California was calling his name.

It just wasn't calling mine.

He thought I'd be eager to join him in California. I'd be closer to Mom and childhood friends. And life wouldn't be such a struggle. There'd be fewer attempted phone robberies and subway mouth fishhookings. Maybe we could even get a dog and a place with a yard. It all sounded pleasant six months prior when he first brought up the move.

But then it stopped sounding pleasant.

I wasn't ready to stop chasing my own goals and felt that we could withstand the pangs of long distance once more. A little more long distance never killed anyone. My new therapist, who I'd been seeing about a year prior to Ben's move, said I was purposefully self-sabotaging.

Ben wanted me to join him in California, and career aside, I interpreted joining him as an implicit decision to get married. He'd made it clear that he wasn't putting that pressure on me, though: "I don't want to marry you, you nut," he'd said with a smile. But even so, through therapy, I saw my fear of marriage routinely come up.

I felt I only had two paths: choosing my career, or choosing marriage.

Marriage was a new fear.

Somewhere during my very healthy and rewarding relationship with Ben, marriage became my "death," in that it was the topic that sent me to my dark place. I was finally living freely, away from Mom and away from Los Angeles. Marriage felt like the end to that. It had nothing to do with my belief in Ben—we were fully committed to each other in every way—but opting to bring the law into our relationship felt fatal. It marked an inescapable ending rather than a hopeful beginning. I already had the love I wanted.

As a child I never played with dolls; I never had pretend conversations with plastic figurines about fake marriages or fairytale endings. Life was real to me. All of it. Every moment. So I never aspired to find a prince or get married.

When marriage became a topic I'd get hit with often, I decided it meant my youth was over. It meant that my dream of living independently would have to end. Not because I couldn't sleep with anyone else but Ben, but because there would be nothing else in life to look forward to. No more growth moments. No more learning. Signing up for marriage would bring me that much closer to the thing I spent my life avoiding: death.

My therapist worked with me on this tirelessly, trying to understand why my perception of marriage was so dark. My parents were happily married, so that wasn't it.

We never came to a conclusion.

I looked at Ben who was standing in our bedroom by the window.

"I know. Who's going to protect me from muggers now?" I asked him quite seriously, responding to his water-under-the-window-sill joke.

He tried his best to crack an authentic smile.

I'd spent those months debating whether or not to go with Ben to the West Coast, suffocated by my own internal dialogue, which flip-flopped between thinking I owed it to myself to continue fighting for my career in New York, and hanging up my hopes of becoming a great editor and moving to Silicon Valley to be a great girlfriend.

Or wife.

The closer the time came for Ben to leave, the more of an emotional disaster I became, surrounding myself with 22-year-olds at work because I viewed them as uncomplicated birds. Their day-to-day pressures weren't heavy, at least in my eyes, so I suffocated my inability to cope with Ben leaving by ignoring it. While Ben was packing up his things in the apartment and looking to spend quality time with me, I was kicking back glasses of Jameson and Ginger Ale, learning about millennial culture from the millennials themselves.

I found the advice everyone gave me to be shitty at best. People that thought I should go said "If you let him go, just know the relationship will end." And people that wanted me to stay said "You can't leave New York, this is where your life is now. You are living your dream." The remarks couldn't have felt more generic; they could have applied to just about anyone.

I'd quit my job at *LA Livin'* and moved to Manhattan over three and a half years before Ben announced he was moving, and spent the majority of that time in New York getting dicked around by editors and human resource specialists. The first job I had in New York was at WPNI, Washington Post Newsweek Interactive, working part time as a Style Editor for a brand new eco-friendly website. But since that position never had the funding of WPNI to become full time, I left when an opportunity at a flashy regional magazine opened up. But then I was laid off there after six months, the day before Thanksgiving. After that I went on unemployment and was quickly hired off-the-books by a photo editor at *Maxim* magazine. She was getting ready to fire the current photo assistant and thought I'd be perfect, so she brought me in for three interviews. She finalized the role over the phone and gave me a start date. Three days before I was slated to show up, the photo editor got fired and out with her went my offer. From there, I took freelance jobs at magazines wherever I could get them.

One time I was up for a really big job at *Health* magazine. I couldn't believe it when they brought me in. On my first interview at *Health*, the editor told me that she didn't want to interview me until I took the edit test. An edit test was essentially a massive homework assignment, where you'd have anywhere from 24 hours to a few days to write articles, edit articles, pitch ideas, critique pages, and solve various problems. And it had to be error-proof.

The editor handed me a red folder with 10 pieces of paper inside. I took it home and opened it up. It was intimidating. I needed to edit 2,000 words and deliver a full page of notes, write three 250-word stories, critique a section of the magazine, and pitch a variety of different ideas. The editor told me that they didn't want to open the position up to non-Time Inc. employees, which meant me, but since the applicants she'd met with were so underwhelming she had no choice.

She brought me in two more times after I submitted my edit test, and on the second time she met me in the waiting room barefoot, which I interpreted as a good sign. She hadn't bothered to put her shoes on, she must have already considered me a colleague.

We spoke candidly about the position. She thought I was fantastic. And surprised, given that I didn't go to Columbia School of Journalism or intern at Condé Nast or Hearst. She told me that they had narrowed it down to two people: me and a Beauty Editor from *Glamour*. She was going to bring us both in to meet with the Editor-in-Chief.

They never brought me back in, and in typical editorial fashion, they never reached out to me to explain that they'd hired the other woman. It was only because I dug around on the internet that I learned the girl from *Glamour* got the gig. I was crushed. Interviewing someone barefoot meant nothing.

In my three and a half years in New York, the city had

broken my heart time and time again, but I was also used to it and kept networking and pitching stories, trying to meet as many editors as I possibly could. I went to events by myself and connected dots better than anyone else. If an editor joined a new magazine, that meant that her old job was open. I just had to apply for it in a tactical way. The first step was to open up the magazine and find out who that editor's boss was. Then I'd email him or her directly, as though I were part of the inner-circle of journalists. If there was a connection I could draw, I would. I'd never lie about who I knew—that was a line I just wouldn't cross—but I'd make sure that I had as much leverage as possible. Condé Nast, Hearst, and Time Inc. were all nepotistic companies. Once you were in, you were in. I just had to get in.

I finally got my big break at MTV.

While the network wasn't in the traditional publishing business, it was one of the largest media companies in the world, and they were hiring an Associate Editor to report on television and entertainment. After reaching out to a publicist friend that I knew in Los Angeles, I was able to connect with someone at MTV and get an interview. A face-to-face interview with a major editor. And she wanted me.

Holy fucking shit.

The MTV job was full-time freelance, which, after the magazine crash of 2008, was the norm. Full time headcount roles were all getting replaced with full-time freelancer ones, but the jobs were the same so I didn't care. I only cared about the cool stuff I'd get to write and who I'd be writing it for—my soon-to-be boss came from *Teen People*. It was surreal.

MTV offered me $40,000 a year, and while I wanted more for my ego, it was plenty. I could pay my half of the rent—Ben and I split up our rent equally, paying $1,250 each—and still have an entire check left. Everyone I knew in New York put at least half of their salary toward rent, so it was right inline with them.

I zipped around MTV's Times Square office like I'd won the lottery, saying "yes" to every single assignment my editor threw my way. I was tasked with writing six stories per day, sometimes interviewing reality stars from shows like *The Hills* and *Jersey Shore*, other times about stuff that was slightly less ridiculous.

My team was small: myself, an Editorial Assistant, and my Managing Editor. We worked closely with show producers, creating content that would drive TV viewers to MTV. com. So following an episode of *The Real World*, a commercial would nudge you to visit MTV.com to get more exclusive content. Written by me. Or my team.

I was deeply embedded in the world of television, specifically MTV's reality programing. If *Jersey Shore's* Snooki fell in the sand at the beach because she was drunk and wearing high heels, I was plugged in and on, typing away at my computer in my cubicle on the 17th floor of the famous Viacom building at

1515 Broadway. Giving my insider take on the matter, writing it like I was her friend. That was the angle we always took, and I enjoyed writing that way.

When Ben said he was moving to Silicon Valley, I'd only been at MTV for eight months. I'd just broken "into" the network. I'd just arrived in some sense. I couldn't leave it.

Not yet, anyway.

I wanted people to understand why I wasn't leaving New York. I told them that I couldn't just get any job in Silicon Valley because I just finally nabbed a great editing job at MTV in New York with smart people and I fought so long to get there and that I couldn't just walk away from that and that MTV San Francisco was purely a gaming office so, no, I couldn't just transfer there like I worked at Peet's Coffee or something. I told them that I couldn't write about technology because I understood nothing about it, so there'd be no jobs in Silicon Valley for me unless I wanted to go work on an iPhone app or write copy for a company blog. And I didn't want to do that because I wanted to become a real writer. Even though I was writing about reality TV stars like Snooki and documenting the intimate details of her self-tanning empire, I was getting somewhere. I was climbing. I was four months away from getting my own business card with the damn MTV logo on it. I wasn't working for a sister brand like Comedy Central or VH1.

I was at the mothership.

Love would have to wait.

There were thousands of deep, wonderful things about my relationship with Ben, but I had no faith in what would happen to us—or me—when he left. Even though we both wanted to stay together, I would most likely crumble to pieces and wail my heart out in his absence, and that looming truth—that looming anxiety—was toxic. But I knew, somewhere buried in my childish brain, that I could not give in to the terror.

It wasn't about whether I thought our love could handle the six-hour flights and countless missed calls, and it wasn't about whether I believed our bond had the juice to go the distance, either. It was about whether I believed that I was tough enough to stay in New York alone without him.

And I didn't.

Which is exactly why I had to try.

"Stop explaining yourself to people," Ben said a few weeks leading up to his departure. He was on the couch, fiddling with a Rubik's Cube. He especially liked the annoying rattling sound it made when he rotated the layers. "I love you and we will make this work. I believe in you and we are both making good decisions to advance our careers, so you believe in us too." He put the cube down and gave me a knowing expression.

I exhaled sharply through my nose. Great insight, coming from the person I was electing not to move with.

"Everyone thinks you will find someone else in California and that I'll end up alone in the suburbs with a cat, and I hate cats," I told him.

"Who said that?"

No one had. I said it.

I believed that Ben was going to move to the tech capital of the world and change the face of education and win awards and be recognized for his work and start playing the guitar and learn to grow vegetables in his yard because he'd have a garden made with fresh compost and, because I didn't go with him, find some gorgeous girl that worked for the Sierra Club and thought, like he did, that New York City was too congested and too expensive and packed with people who never actually achieved anything because they were always busy finding themselves. I feared that Ben and his Sierra Club princess would go on bike rides along the coast in Toms slip-on shoes because they gave back to the world, and they'd host truffle oil parties for their friends and they'd all sit around their long dining room table that was made of reclaimed wood from Yosemite. And I hated that thought especially because the Ben I knew never cooked.

"I dunno, maybe no one said that, but people are suggesting that you won't wait forever and that I'm fucking up by staying here." It wasn't the first time we'd had that talk. It always started and ended the same way.

He picked the cube back up and rattled it, rotating the layers faster than before.

"You need to think about what's happening on the other

end of the phone when you call your friends and ask for advice. They're probably watching TV and painting their nails and just regurgitating something they saw on *Oprah* that in no way actually applies to our lives," he said.

It was hard to pay attention to him with the Rubik's Cube in his hand.

"Can you put that down?"

His nostrils flared. "Are you even listening to me?"

"Yes, but that cube thing is so annoying."

He shook his head. "Not to be a jerk, but you're naïve if you honestly believe that these people are invested in your life the way that I or your parents are."

Not that my friends were assholes, but aren't all friends, more or less, assholes? Let's say, for example, Jasmine doesn't know if she should move to Australia or stay in San Francisco. When Jasmine calls Melissa to talk it over, Melissa's got her own shit to deal with and picking out Jasmine's zip code is not high on her priority list. Melissa cares about Jasmine's happiness, no doubt, but Melissa's immediate goal is to end the chat as soon as possible so she can finish making that panini that's about to burn. Melissa is listening to her friend but is focused on that 'nini. Melissa has to make a quick decision so she shoves worried Jasmine off the phone by reassuring her that "everything is going to work out." And then Jasmine gets off the call confused because she just called her very best friend in the world and she can't for the life of her understand why

Melissa didn't make her feel any better, and now Jasmine's more lost than ever.

Maybe no one understands poor Jasmine.

Now Jasmine feels completely alone in this world. And really, all that happened was that Jasmine called Melissa in the middle of lunch.

My desire to stay in New York was not just about New York.

I wanted to do the anti-Michigan thing. I wanted to know that I had grown enough as a person and that I was capable of doing something that would have absolutely terrified me 11 years earlier.

But Mom said I was doing the exact same thing as Michigan.

"Are you sure you're not making this decision out of fear?"

"Well, I am. I am terrified, so I am choosing to do the terrifying thing."

"I don't see it that way."

I didn't want to believe her, though, because I knew deep down she wanted me back in California for her own benefit.

Staying behind in a city alone was going to scare the living shit out of me and probably make me shake and cry in the way that stepping foot on the Wolverine campus did. Ben was my partner. He was my protector, and the easy thing would've been to go where I felt safe and secure, but this was my one opportunity to do the scary thing that Beki would never have been able to do.

Much like the way Mom separated Margaret from Samantha, I wanted to break off my ties with Beki. It was time for Rebecca to take over and face the scary thing.

The girl that only lasted at University of Michigan for 24 hours would have never survived Manhattan alone; she would've become hysterical and sprinted after familiar love. I had to stay and do this for her.

So I did.

First I saw my therapist and finally got a prescription for anti-anxiety medication.

But then I stayed.

Beth Israel Hospital ER, New York, Just After Ben Left

"You know you're missing a ramekin from your baking set," Mom said one afternoon while rifling through my cupboards on East 22nd Street. Ben moved out for California nearly three weeks prior to Mom's visit, and I was waiting out our lease.

While most out-of-town parents would visit their kids and take them to dinner or board a double-decker bus for a city tour, mine would come with suitcases overflowing with Costco trash bags, because I couldn't possibly be expected to find those in New York. She'd also pack dish sponges because they also "didn't sell those in New York," and on occasion, she'd bring chef's knives, although I have no idea how she was allowed to fly with them. Then, after unpacking her smorgasbord of membership-only by-the-bulk loot, she'd spend the rest of the afternoon whipping up fantastic Italian dishes on my tiny electric stove while scouring the halls for my superintendent to tell him what a great job he was doing but could he please arrange to have someone spray my apartment for bugs.

Even with all of that distraction—the unpacking and cooking and the pointing out of the insects—she noticed the one missing dish in my cabinet.

"It doesn't matter—no one is coming over for meals," I said dropping my head.

"Well it's just silly. You only have three here. Are you going to complete the set or just have a hodgepodge of dishware? What is a person supposed to make with just three?"

The same thing I made with four—nothing.

"I don't care—Ben's gone and I'm moving out in a month anyway," I snapped. "I'm getting rid of all of this stuff."

I did not want to tell her what happened to the other porcelain baking dish she bought me.

"You broke it, didn't you? Well that would imply that you actually used it. Tell me what you made!" Her voice was packed with so much enthusiasm she sounded like a game show host. *Well, Dan, tell them what you made!* For those few moments, my mother's dreams had come true: she'd spawned a little chef. She stepped away from the stove and looked at me for an answer.

Why was Mom intent on cracking the desert dish whodunit? This was New York City, some people didn't even have functioning ovens because they opted to shut off the gas in favor of storage space. *Time Out New York* ran an entire article on the phenomenon, actually, birthing the grossly idiotic yet appropriate colloquialism, *kitchenista*. So many people were storing their clothing in the kitchen that they had to come up with a word for it. The fact that I even *had* serving pieces in my cupboard and not '60s-inspired mohair sweaters from Housing Works thrift store already legitimized my kitchen.

I stuck my face right in front of Mom's. "Can we please drop it?"

What really happened to the ramekin:

Ben moved out of our apartment a few weeks before Mom's visit, and to no one's surprise, I shriveled into an emotional wet rag.

He found a guy on some bidding website to move all of his things to California, and woke up one morning and loaded up the truck. Most of our furniture was cheap so he didn't bother taking any of it with him. So off he went with his clothing, computers, ski gear, and bike. I was looped in with every step and every decision that Ben was making, mostly because he wanted me to know how much he wanted me to join him, but still, when he actually left, it hit me in total surprise.

Ben left on a Monday morning. Before my coffee could even finish brewing, the moving truck showed up and practically looted our apartment. After the boxes and bike vanished there was nothing but our blank walls and shitty furniture, which was all destined for Craigslist or the curb.

I immediately went to work to distract myself. That evening, for the first time in a long time, I walked home from my Times Square office. Leisurely. Both excited at this new city that I hoped to conquer, and apathetic because there was no one at East 22nd Street waiting for me when I got home.

The following night Mom called from California. "My third cousin's daughter is moving to New York, I told her it would be okay if she stayed in your apartment."

"Wait, what?"

"She just graduated college and is moving from Florida. She needs a place to stay until she gets a job," Mom explained.

I was alone in the apartment and wanted the company—even with my fast-acting prescription benzos. "Fine," I said quickly.

Mom's third cousin once removed showed up on Friday, and she was a pleasant distraction.

The weekend came and went, and on Monday, seven days after Ben left our apartment, I started experiencing severe upper abdominal pain. It felt like tiny hands were jabbing tiny knives right below my breasts. Hundreds of little punctures, like a tattoo needle. I knew it wasn't menstrual cramps because of how high up the stabbing was.

I sucked it up for about a day and tried to distract myself from the discomfort with Aleve, but the miniature knife jabs continued.

Stab.

Stab.

Slash.

I couldn't take it anymore. I opened my laptop and consulted the holy grail of self-diagnosing, WebMD, and decided that, after frantically reading through each page, I should go see a doctor.

I called Ben. "It's really bad and it's been 24 hours," I moaned.

"Yes, just go to the hospital already," he said firmly. "Can your Mom's cousin go with you?"

"Good idea."

We hung up, but before I left for the hospital I wanted to call Mom.

"So do you think I should go to the hospital?" I asked. I was hoping to get a "yes" from her.

"Honey, do you think this is just your anxiety?" she asked.

"It can't be."

The pain in my body was different than anxiety.

But with every moment I spent fixated on the little hands with the little knives, I added to the agony, like a stew. First with shaking, then the chills, then trips to the bathroom. While I wanted to ignore Mom's over-the-phone diagnosis, she was half right. I was self-aware enough to know what the beginning of a panic attack looked like—my neck hurt, I was freezing cold—and this was it.

On the phone with Mom I was quiet, listening, hunched over at the foot of my bed, which was barren now since Ben had taken his wretched comforter with him.

"Come home," she said, soothingly. Her voice felt like a massage on my stomach. The little hands with the little knives ran for cover when Mom spoke. "I'll make you meatballs, and anything else you want."

But then in a split-second her words sounded ugly. Her advice equally as such. The panic that had been seesawing between mild and intense just commited to go full force, and she wasn't helping.

I hung up the phone and ran back into the bathroom. I was experiencing acute abdominal stress and started to cough. A lot. Then my chest felt weird, not panic-weird, but like someone was punching me in the sternum. The little hands had dropped their knives and were now resorting to using their fists.

I scurried out of the bathroom on high alert and found my distant relative in her bedroom watching Netflix on her laptop. I didn't know anything about her—we'd literally just met days prior and only gotten through the customary basics—but I had no choice. I had to ask her for help. I needed her.

"Hey," I started. "My chest really hurts and the pain isn't going away. I know it's late, but Ben thinks I should go to a hospital, do you think you'd come with me?" I said, wiping a small bit of sweat from my brow.

She tossed her laptop to the side and got up from her air mattress.

I'd never given any thought to New York City hospitals... except for one time on a bus when a middle-aged man sat next to me and explained how he and his hat, which read Bellevue Hospital, were one of the few remnants of the old psychiatric ward. Something I never thought about again until I decided at 12:10 a.m. that I should Google the closest hospitals. It was between Bellevue or Beth Israel. By that time the pain had been partially dampened by my raging anxiety, so I picked the hospital that was closest.

I trotted six blocks down 1st Avenue to Beth Israel Hospital with my distant cousin, now my savior, at my side. While still a total stranger, her presence was reassuring.

I'd live. Maybe.

I expected New York to be pitch black outside, more ominous than usual given that's how I believed frightening hospital adventures should appear, but it looked like every night. The Dunkin' Donuts on the corner was still open, and there was a huge truck unloading boxes of groceries into Gristedes market, right on schedule.

I walked fast with short steps, holding my stomach with just one hand the way someone might do while dancing.

Or dying.

I stepped inside of Beth Israel and squinted. I found a

guard at intake and gave him just enough information so he could determine whether or not I was in the right place. He pointed to a row of brown plastic chairs and told me to take a seat. There was a man sprawled across five of them, so I let him sleep and found a bench far off in the corner.

I texted Ben. My hands shook. "Made it to hospital. It's gross. Am okay."

A nurse finally called my name and walked me through big double doors and into the ER area. She pointed at a teal green cot and told me to take a seat, before running an EKG test on me to make sure I wasn't having a heart attack and then stabbing my vein with a fat needle for the IV. Then she disappeared behind a curtain.

I'd never had a problem with needles before, but the IV needle one hurt almost as bad as my chest. I looked at my left arm, which was turning an ominous shade of blue.

"Does this look right?" I asked my third cousin once removed, who was doing her best to stay alert by playing games on her phone.

She shrugged.

An hour passed and no one had come to check on me. My inner elbow where the nurse had jabbed the needle started to throb and the pain coursed through my bones.

I heard a nurse talking a few cots down so I yelled to her. "Can anyone help me?" My voice was meek and breathy. "My arm is blue."

"It's a busy night for us. Got a lot of withdrawals to deal with," the voice echoed back.

I looked at my phone which had been lying next to me on the cot. The screen said it was nearly 3:00 a.m.

I flagged down the next nurse I could see. "Can you please take the IV out of my arm?" I whined, holding back tears. The pain had become so severe that I couldn't move my fingers. They were limp.

The nurse waved me off. "Be there in just a second."

Seconds passed. Then minutes.

"Can you see if you can find a blanket?" I asked my cousin.

At 4:00 a.m. I flailed in my cot, side to side so that it would squeak. I was in complete agony. Finally, the nurse appeared.

"I'm so sorry none of the doctors have been in yet, but your EKG is normal so that's good," she said cheerfully. She looked at my arm. "Yeah, it's a little blue," she noted. "That happens." Then she yanked the IV out of my arm like she was pulling a plug out of the socket, and walked away.

I'd been stewing in my own grief for hours, oscillating between being fixated on my gut-wrenching stomach pain and worried that I was just panicking and experiencing anxiety in a new form. That my awareness of Ben's absence, coupled with Mom's discouraging words, were what had brought me to this hell hole of a hospital, and it was only my numb, semi-paralyzed arm that enabled me to focus my attention on something real.

My arm—which I was convinced would almost certainly fall off if I remained in the hospital—grounded me, and I went from panicking about my stomach to being present and livid.

I pushed myself upright and rested my feet on the floor. "Let's get out of here," I said to my cousin.

We marched out.

The following morning I called in sick to work at MTV, then phoned my general doctor. She was out of the office, but her nurse recommended I see a gastroenterologist and gave me the name of one in New York. My cousin had a job interview in the morning, so I went alone.

The gastroenterologist examined me, asked me a number of questions about my diet and recent behavior, and then had a nurse come in to tell me about the next steps. I was so tired and consumed with self-pity that I hadn't listened to anything she said.

Minutes later, a different nurse walked in holding an empty jar in her hands.

"So, Dr. Vhyshik explained that she'd like you to leave a sample, but you can do this at home, you don't have to do it here."

"Oh, I'm going back home now?"

She rolled her eyes. "Well, yes you have to go home. She wants you back this afternoon for your procedure."

"Wait, what? Sorry, I didn't catch that with Dr. Vhyshik,"

I said clenching my teeth. "A procedure?"

The word "procedure" echoed in my ears.

The nurse flooded my brain with instructions, none of which I could tether myself to. My mind swirled and my nerves clacked. What was this nurse even saying? Not understanding her was becoming monumentally terrifying. I was floating in a thick cloud of confusion.

Then, she said one word that brought me back to life: enema.

I was going to give myself an enema.

The nurse placed a small blue box into my lap and explained that as soon as I got home I'd need to inject an entire bottle of liquid into my backend…myself.

"Just follow the diagrams on the side of the box," she said.

I rotated the carton and spotted an illustration of two people lying in Kama Sutra-like positions on the floor. The enema box artist never bothered to fill in their facial expressions. That struck me as particularly alarming. And not that it mattered, but I didn't understand why the illustration suggested that this was a two-person gig.

"And, can you tell me what procedure I'm having? I'd like to write it down," I asked. The adult in me took control.

"An endoscopy and a flex sig," she answered.

I scribbled those unfamiliar words down onto a piece of paper so I could call Dad and tell him. She shuffled me in the direction of a check-out nurse, seated in a cubicle behind a big sheet of glass. I sat in front of her.

"You'll be under anesthesia so is there someone that will be able to pick you up," she asked, robotically, from behind the sheet of glass.

"Um, no," I whispered. "I'm," I paused. "I'm alone." I sank in the chair.

Part of me expected her to care. To slide open the glass that separated us and hold my hand. But she didn't even blink.

"We can connect you with a company that will get you home safely." Then she handed me a business card.

I left the office with a plastic bag of ass trinkets and called my parents.

"I have to go under anesthesia and I don't have anybody to pick me up," I wailed hysterically into the phone while walking home. "I have no one."

Then I read them the names of the procedures I was slated to have. Dad wanted the name and number of the doctor so he could call. He said it sounded drastic and wanted to make sure that I was in the best care. Since I hadn't actually hung onto any of the information I'd been given, he wanted to call for himself.

"Thanks, Dad," I slobbered into the phone. I was planning to take a cab back home to my apartment on 22nd Street, but I couldn't think clearly so I just continued walking, hysterically sobbing. The sidewalk was filled with people, but no one noticed me—what I both loved and hated about New York.

I put my key in the door, set my (s)tool kit on the kitchen table, and took a seat on a Rubbermaid step stool. After Ben moved out, I decided that when our lease ended I would relocate to an apartment in the East Village—a neighborhood that always seemed more my speed than sleepy Gramercy—so once he left, the first thing I did in preparation of that was sell all of our chairs on Craigslist. At that moment, seated on a Rubbermaid step stool with an enema and poop scoop looming over me, I wished I hadn't done that.

My butt wanted a real chair.

With less than 30 minutes to complete two embarrassing tasks, I went to the bathroom and sat on the toilet. Next to me, an army of termites crawled out of a wall pipe and marched into the tub.

I held the empty container underneath my butt in the toilet and sat patiently. I wearily thought about the following assignment—the enema—and wondered if the faceless people on the side of the box had a much larger bathroom and whether they had insects breeding in their tub at the time.

Then, before I could stop what was happening, I stood up from the toilet and saw that I mistakenly contaminated the jar with my pee.

"Fuck!" I screamed. I was supposed to poop in it. Without a second container to gather anything in or any time to spare,

I bolted out of the bathroom and grabbed the first dish-like item I could find.

I returned to the bathroom, completed the task of collecting my poop, and moved onto the enema portion of my homework. I got onto my knees and did what the instructions said, staring at the swarming army of termites belly-flopping into my tub. *I'll deal with them later,* I thought.

I emptied my insides, grabbed my specimen sample, and headed back out to 1st Avenue, grabbing the first cab I could find.

~~~~~~~~~

Oh, so the ramekin. Yeah, I crapped in it. It was the nicest thing Dr. Vhyshik ever had shit delivered in.

222 East 3rd Street, East Village, 2012

Clostridium difficile, or C. diff, as Dr. Vhyshik called it when she phoned me at home days later, was fucking disgusting, in every way that one might expect a bacterial intestinal infection would be. The diarrhea was unending, with a stench so putrid it smelled more like animal manure than anything a human could produce.

From the hallway my Ben-less apartment appeared level with the ground floor, but once you opened the door, three small steps led you down to my actual unit. I sat on the cold wooden second step, still with no chairs in my apartment, resting both a piece of paper and my elbow on my knee.

"Can you spell that so that I can look it up?" I asked Dr. Vhyshik. "And the d is lowercase?"

The letter d and the weird spacing just added to the confusion.

"So," I paused, "How did I get this?"

"Typically it affects hospital patients," she responded.

My brain went static. *I'd been to a hospital!* In that moment I had a hard time believing that I would have contracted "Capital C period space lowercase diff" in the short time I was admitted at Beth Israel.

My thoughts swirled around, organizing the chain of events like an investigator piecing together a crime. I went to the hospital *after* the pain in my abdomen started, that part I knew. But I still didn't understand when I contracted it. Had I gone to the ER with simple anxiety, and then developed a real illness while I was there? And if so, did that mean that after all my wishful thinking about what I could accomplish on my own in New York City, anxiety— and Mom—beat me again?

My lease finally expired and it was time to finally leave my apartment and relocate to the East Village.

Committed to the plan to stay in New York after Ben left, I moved 19 blocks south and a few avenues over into an apartment in the East Village, at 222 East 3rd Street. Technically it was called Alphabet City. My building was nestled next to a community garden and Avenue B. Proximity to Avenue B was an important factor in determining how comfortable I felt in a neighborhood with prominent tenement buildings. I took note of their locations at Avenue C and Avenue D, and felt good about how close I was to Avenue B.

Visually the apartment was perfect, with exposed brick walls, hardwood floors, and a shared renovated roof deck with 360-degree views of the city. I moved in with two girls I'd met on Craigslist. It was a two-bedroom apartment, but they'd converted the living room into a third. So even though the rent was a soaring $4,000, we each paid $1,333. A steal.

My two new roommates, Kelly and Meredith, were both in nursing school at NYU, which was a huge win, as it meant they'd be able to complete important roommate duties like performing CPR on me and examining my mouth with a tongue depressor.

One of the first things I shared about myself when I moved in was my experience at Beth Israel.

"Oh no, always go to NYU," my new roommate Kelly said, as though this was something I should have known.

My bedroom on East 3rd Street was a writer's dream, with huge glass windows that looked over the building's private garden. It was quiet and filled with natural light, so I wrote in my room often, locking the door and only coming out for bathroom or coffee breaks.

Weeks after moving in I got the biggest freelance assignment of my career: a blurb in *Time Out New York*. I'd joined a non-profit and spent many weekends volunteering and networking as part of it. Because of that, I connected with a volunteer that was also an editor at *Time Out New York*. And because of that editor, I got my first huge assignment: a 100-

word piece about political volunteer opportunities in New York City. It would require tons of research and pay me $75. As much as I wanted to get out on the weekends and explore the East Village, I happily locked myself in my new bedroom working on that *Time Out New York* assignment.

I wanted Mom to fly out and see my new place. I thought she'd be impressed. Proud of the medically-minded roommates I found, and the vibe of my neighborhood, and that I'd even picked a building with a part-time doorman who would greet me at night and see that I got into the elevator safely.

I asked Mom when she was coming to visit.

"I'm sure your place is fantastic but I just don't think I have another flight to New York in me. I was just there," she answered.

I sighed.

She'd been a terrible flyer her whole life, and while she and I shared that trait, I'd found success in my Ativan dosing. Anti-anxiety medication did nothing for her, though. Once, under a doctor's care, she tried ingesting what she says was a horse tranquilizer's worth of Xanax and was still able to speak clearly and do needlepoint.

"I'll visit you when you move to California," she added, somberly.

I knew Mom didn't want to fly again, but I also felt part of the reason she wouldn't come visit me was because she was deeply disappointed in my choice to stay. She was concerned that Ben would lose patience the longer I remained in New York, and no matter how many times I told her that I was staying to prove to myself and my anxiety that I could be strong, she just saw it otherwise. She saw it as me being scared to do something new.

She saw it as the same old story.

I hated that she felt that way, but when she'd say those words to me—"you're just scared"—it didn't feel wrong, either. I couldn't get myself to truly believe in my motive. Somewhere inside of me I knew she wasn't totally wrong. My idealized self was strong and staying in New York to chase my independence and dreams, that was certain. But my actual self? I had no clue.

The month of my 30th birthday was particularly hard. I knew Ben and my parents would send me something great and call me all day, but it wouldn't change the fact that I felt like an orphan of sorts. There was something I'd always found addicting about feeling sorry for myself, so the concept of being alone on my 30th birthday in New York drew me in quick. There'd be no one waiting for me to get home when I turned 30. No one who really knew my whereabouts; just me and the city I chose.

Still, wanting to celebrate and pick myself up, I convinced two of my best friends from Los Angeles, Julie and Erica, to fly out for my birthday. I didn't have anything planned when they booked their flights, but told them by the time they got to Manhattan I'd have something in the works. Ben told me that he was planning a big trip for us the following month and that the specifics were a surprise.

It was 8:00 p.m. on Friday, the last day of my 20s, when my phone buzzed with a new text message from one of my best friends, Michole: "Let's go to Blind Barber."

Blind Barber had been one of my favorite bars when I moved to New York. During the day, the front of the bar operated as a functioning barber shop, with authentic parlor chairs, glass jars of teal blue Barbicide, and old world charm that reminded me of Grandpa's shop on Jobs Lane in Southampton. At night, though, the back wall of the barber shop slid open to reveal a secret speakeasy-style bar, complete with black-and-white tiled floors, dim lighting, and ripped leather booths that reeked of Jack Daniels. New Yorkers had grown tired of the kitsch and crowd at Blind Barber, which began to skew younger and sloppier, but not me—you couldn't have found a bar that appealed to me more.

A familial barber shop with a secret door? Sold.

I texted Michole back: "In."

Around 11:00 p.m I found her outside. We walked up to Blind Barber and told the enormous doorman with the eye-patch that we knew the guy that ran the place. He checked our IDs and nodded. The secret door in the back of the barber shop was shut, so I grabbed the metal lever and yanked it open.

It was dark and loud inside, per usual, but in the far back corner perched on a leather booth I spotted Julie and Erica in enormous sequined hats.

"What are you guys doing here already?" I squealed, grabbing their wrists firmly. They weren't supposed to arrive until the following day. Then I saw my two roommates, also in massive sparkly cowboy hats. Behind them I saw at least 10 of my good New York friends, who all shouted "surprise!" as loudly as they could.

I clapped my hands together laughing, scanning the sea of friendly faces when, off in the corner next to the DJ booth, I saw a familiar silhouette in a mint green and black flannel shirt, with the top button unbuttoned.

Holy shit it was Ben.

I jumped on him and flung my arms around his neck in a way that was very un-me. I was not a jumper or an arm flinger by any means.

"What are you doing here?" I yelled, pressing my mouth against his ear.

He and Michole planned the whole thing. They told Julie and Erica to come in a day early, and they rallied all my New York friends. Then, because I'd been going through a wide-brimmed black hat obsession, Ben bought dozens of large hats from the party supply store for people to wear.

I spent a few moments wishing I had dressed nicer for the occasion—it was my 30th birthday, after all—but as soon as the Maker's Mark shots came, I grabbed a sequined hat off of someone and tossed it on, tugging on the sides whenever the DJ played a song I liked. At one point I'd collected all the hats I could find, put them on my head, and jumped up on the leather booth to show them off to the crowd. One of the owners yelled at me and told me to come down. "Wait," I said pointing my left hand at him. "Let me finish my drink." Then I jumped down, sending my stack of hats toppling over.

More drinks, more shots, and a few hours later, I was toast. I grabbed Erica and pulled her through the crowd of sweaty dancers toward the front door. I needed to throw up. I ran across the street, hurled my upper body over the metal bars surrounding Tompkins Square Park and vomited directly into the plants.

In between hurls I stood up straight to talk.

"I can't believe all these people are here for me."

I was in awe of the friendships I had formed. All of these people had gathered together at this weird bar in the East Village because they liked me. I wanted to give her a huge hug, but then I tossed my head forward and threw up again. She laughed every time I tried to speak. I was behaving like a sorority girl.

"Just get it all out and then we can talk."

I followed her orders, finished barfing, and gave her the thumbs up to indicate that I was ready to return to the party. We scampered back inside and I marched right back to the dance floor and asked someone for a hat. Mary J. Blige was playing and I needed to dance. Ben was sitting in the booth smiling at me.

"Get it, girl," he shouted, oblivious to where I had been or how I smelled.

At the end of the party Ben told me that he'd gotten us a hotel room at the Thompson right off Houston Street, so I gave Erica and Julie my house keys and went with Ben, stopping along the walk every block or so to dry heave. He laughed at me each time I spit up, and I laughed right back. I smelled absolutely terrible, and the hair surrounding my face was wet with sweat and bits of goop that I was pretty sure wasn't vomit but I still couldn't identify.

Ben grabbed my hand and we strolled down the street toward the hotel. It'd been eight months since he moved away. In the months before he left, I was in a perpetual state of angst, uncertain of our future and of what I wanted. That night, though, filled with just bourbon and bile, I felt light and free. Nothing was trapping me.

"I'm having so much fun with you right now," I said as we shuffled south toward Houston. He smiled and squeezed my hand tighter. I pointed at a bodega on the corner and said that

I was craving cereal. I asked him if he wanted anything.

"Just a water," he said.

I took a step inside the brightly-lit bodega then spun around and ran back out to Ben on the street.

He was standing next to a pile of neatly stacked trash bags. "I bet we can have just as much fun in California," I said, looking up at him.

He laughed through his nose. "Let's talk about this when you're slightly less wasted."

"Who cares that I'm wasted. I can leave New York now. I don't need it anymore." I was on an emotional high. Sure I'd only lasted eight months without Ben but it felt right. Announcing that I was ready to go felt like the right thing to shout. It went against everything sober Rebecca had told him—that I still wasn't ready to leave New York—but on that street next to that pile of garbage, I wanted to pick Ben. I wanted to be spontaneous. I wanted to say goodbye to Rebecca, the girl stuck in a perpetual state of indecision regarding life and her anxiety and her relationship with her mother, and announce that I'd been cured, somehow, and that I was ready to leave my great city.

"Okay then," he said, attempting to placate me with a smile.

I smiled back and walked back into the bodega to buy my favorite drunken late-night snack, a single serving of Honey Nut Cheerios and a carton of milk.

We would commemorate this moment of emotional maturity and sound decision-making by clinking my cereal box and his water bottle together.

When I stepped out of the bodega a minute later empty-handed, Ben's forehead creased.

I shook my head back.

"Ugh," I groaned, kicking an empty plastic bag on the ground. "It's a 10-dollar minimum, fuck it let's just go, I don't even want cereal anymore."

He stood next to the trash with downcast eyes, and I knew why. It wasn't because I was robbing him of sufficient hydration; rather, it was my immediate change in attitude. I'd gone from blithe, able-to-move-anywhere Rebecca, to irritated, carb-deprived Rebecca, and irritated, carb-deprived Rebecca was not moving anywhere.

"I just want to go to bed," I said, sullenly.

"I know."

I was not moving to California, and he knew it.

Not yet, at least.

California, 2013

Ben knew what he was signing up for when he asked me to join him in California, and he was incredibly patient with me, even after my 30th birthday when I told him I wasn't actually ready to leave.

I'd woken up the morning after that birthday knowing that eight months alone in Manhattan wasn't enough, but when, nine, 10, 15 months came and went, I started to wonder what I was waiting for. Some sort of accolade for graduating life? For doing something that every other person in the world does that I'd never been able to do: live alone. Although I wasn't even doing that—I had roommates. Did 15 months alone in New York equate to anything?

I spent every Tuesday at 6:30 p.m. in my therapist's Murray Hill office, which was actually an apartment inside of a massive tower, making things incredibly weird when I left appointments with swollen eyes and had to share the elevator with residents that were headed to the basement gym.

"When will I know I've achieved what I needed to? I'd ask my therapist. "How long until I'm ready to go?""

Life would present me with the answer. It was 17 months.

On month 17 of my self-imposed single-habitation, nothing earth-shattering happened.

There was no moment of clarity, no night in which sleep felt better, in which I didn't run to the bathroom with diarrhea. I was at a random bar in the East Village on a Tuesday night sitting with friends, physically present but listening to no one, when I had an epiphany.

I could do this forever, I thought. Not sit at the bar, but stay in New York. I could seek treatment for anxiety forever. I could continue to hate sleep and continue to hate aloneness and be co-dependent on Mom, and there would never be a moment in my life in which these things were going to leave me. These things were harnessed to me for the long haul, and they were not going to disappear.

I set my Jameson and Ginger on the table, kissed my friends good night, and walked home in the darkness.

There wasn't a single particle in my body that wanted to untie myself from New York City, and that's why I had to.

A month later I put in my notice at MTV.

Two weeks after that I moved to Silicon Valley, California.

It was an anticlimactic departure. There were no group hugs, no epic goodbyes. Just as when I'd arrived, it was only me.

With all of my friends still out in Montauk enjoying the remaining hours of a perfect Labor Day weekend, I ended up in the city alone. I hailed a cab alone, got in alone, and sat quietly in the back, staring out of the steamy windows into the gray muggy air.

The city was empty, so we breezed through downtown and onto the Williamsburg Bridge, where I closed my eyes, gulped, and felt the burn in my eyes as I thought about everything I was leaving. And possibly losing.

Leaving was hard, but leaving alone carried a heaviness. I'd given the city so much meaning. I foolishly wanted to see the Statue of Liberty cry for me as I crossed into Brooklyn one final time.

She didn't even notice.

~~~~~~~~~~~

Once in California, the angst and emptiness I thought I'd feel over leaving New York never came. Sure, I hated how early restaurants and bars closed, the nonexistence of live music in my new neighborhood of Palo Alto, but I had control.

And I had me.

And for the first time in my entire life, me started to feel like enough. Me got me to JFK. Me got me on that plane. It was me that got all those New York jobs and was fishhooked and almost robbed and almost subway-shanked. I didn't need Mom's safety pamphlet to remain safe, and I didn't need her seal of approval to make decisions.

I was perfectly capable of doing it all myself, and I'd just proven that by moving to California. A place I never thought I'd come back to without kicking and screaming. I was there, smiling and in love.

By choice.

It took me four months to find work. I was hired as an editor at a fashion tech company based in Mountain View, California. I was ecstatic to find a job with the word editor in it.

In December of 2012, four months after relocating, I met a man named STORM who read *X-Men* tarot cards. I always suspected that when it came time for me to really understand my life, a member of the psychic world would be attached to the experience. It was just weird enough that it made sense.

I'd never had a reading before, I wasn't sure I even believed in them, but I was at a work event and convinced myself that everything would turn out okay because complimentary readings were dismissible. If he said something egregious, I'd just wave him off.

STORM took some time getting his miniature statues and other various accoutrements ready outside of the company party, so I scribbled my name down on a sign-up sheet and fetched a drink at the open bar. I ordered all the Jameson and Gingers a gal could get her hands on without offending coworkers (spoiler: it's three) and waited impatiently for my turn.

I exchanged small talk with out of town salespeople. I typically had no qualms with mindless chatter, but on that night, I found my eyes gazing over their shoulders as they spoke, monitoring the table action outside and waiting to hear someone announce my name.

It was finally my turn.

"Please, sit down," STORM said, gesturing at the empty chair in front of him. I obliged quietly because I was officially tipsy and did not want him to think less of me. He was a medium-sized, middle-aged man with a gentle voice, but he wore an absurdly tall hat with a huge brim that made it hard to take him seriously. Who could concentrate on their imminent awakening when a massive hat was masking their psychic's features? Did he even have a nose? I was confused, both by STORM's clothing and why I was giving that moment with him so much meaning.

So when STORM told me to sit down, I did just that.

He asked me to shuffle the tarot deck and select five cards.

I followed orders. Intellectually I knew that there would be pictures on the tarot cards, but I still cocked my head to the side when he displayed them. I couldn't make sense of the illustrations, which I guess was the point, otherwise everyone would be a tarot card reader and STORM would be out of a job.

He placed my selected cards in front of me, sighing just

loud enough for me to hear as he turned over the ones that were facing the wrong direction.

"You have three upside-down cards in the same family," he said, as though that meant something to me. His voice was soft so I leaned in closely to make sure I wouldn't miss anything. "This one here, it represents happiness."

"So I'm happy?" I proposed, unsure as to whether I had just made a statement or asked a question.

"When it faces the wrong way, it could mean that your perception of joy is narrow and clouded."

I stared at the table and blinked. So a few cards were upside down, the mathematical probability of that was high.

But then something inside of me changed course. I became instantly hooked the same way you might when someone reads your horoscope from a magazine and it's frighteningly accurate. Soon you believe all magazine psychics are trusted sources of guidance and you subscribe to an entire year's worth of *Fish & Gully* because that's where The Astro Gals publish their monthly predictions.

I was entranced by STORM and his remarks. He pointed to another card.

"This one represents success."

"So I'm successful?" I asked with a confident smile.

"Well, similar to the last card, you have a narrow definition of what success is. It's flipped."

He changed his focus and looked up at me.

"Honestly, that's kind of right," I said quietly. I needed to explain myself. I did have a muddy view of my achievements. "I used to think success meant I had to become a great editor," I scooted my chair closer to him. "I've always been searching for the next thing that could finally make me happy. Man, I sound so whiny right now," I said, whining.

He said nothing and returned his focus downward at the table. I looked down too, realizing how much pressure I was putting on the table with my body.

I moved onto money because surely he'd agree that my financial unhappiness was marginally validated. Before moving to California to be with Ben I'd been living in a small two-bedroom apartment in the East Village with three people (four if you counted my then-roommate's then-boyfriend) and a 45-pound dog. My parents still paid my cell phone bill. I spent 70 percent of my income on rent alone. I went to stupid parties just so I could fill my belly with lukewarm sliders and promotional vodka. I was nowhere close to getting a "You go, girlfriend," from Suze Orman.

Finally, STORM became interested in the conversation and spoke up.

"And now?"

I let out a long exhale. He was a man of few words. I answered and told him that I'd recently given all that up—the editorial job at the recognized media company in the best city in America in the coolest neighborhood, all illustrated by an impressive Instagram feed—moved 3,000 miles away to a city not conducive to journalism, all to follow something horrifying: love.

"I didn't want to leave New York. It was my home. I had a great job at MTV. It made me feel safe and happy." I continued, telling STORM—a total stranger and a strange one at that—about my battles with anxiety and how New York was the only place I felt I belonged. "Leaving it meant I'll only have love now."

"Maybe you have been happy all along," he said, grinning. "Happy there and happy here."

"No, no. I was *unhappy* before."

He was wrong about me. He didn't get it.

"I only found joy when I moved to New York, don't you see?"

He stared back at me deeply in silence.

I scooted my chair back, digging the legs into the cement. I was about to walk away when he motioned me to lean forward.

I sat back down smiling. *This is it*, I thought. He was going to tell me that he'd lived in New York too. That he spent his entire life running and hiding just as I had, and it was the great city of New York that had welcomed him with open arms. STORM was going to solve my perpetual zip code riddle and set me free. He had the secret sauce to do it, I just felt it in my bones.

"Here, take my business card," he said, handing me a small card with cartoon drawings on it. "You should follow me on Twitter."

I went inside and saw Ben walk into the party. He pulled me in and kissed the top of my head. He pointed out the big sign that said Psychic Readings by STORM and laughed.

"I know," I told him. "I just got a reading done actually, but the guy was a total idiot."

It wasn't until days later, when I was sitting up in bed with my head pressed back against a chilly feather pillow and Ben was sound asleep next to me, taking up a majority of mattress real estate as he often did, that I thought about STORM. At the time of my reading I wrote him off as annoying and obtuse, but maybe he was onto me.

For my entire life I had felt like a runner stuck in the mud. As a kid I did my best to escape Mom and Santa Monica, whether it was by moving to Michigan or traveling to France in seventh grade, and it was my fear—my lack of faith in myself—that always brought me back.

Then when I did manage to move away later in my 20s and relocate to New York City, I found the same weakness that I did in Los Angeles. When Ben asked me to come to California I couldn't leave New York either.

Not because of Mom.

Not because of my anxiety.

But because of me.

The panic attack I had the day I told Ben I wouldn't be moving with him to California was no different than the one I had the afternoon I told my parents that I had to get back on a plane with them and leave the University of Michigan. Cities and parents weren't concocting the gravitational pull toward unhappiness, it was me.

It was the power I gave my anxiety and the way I let myself become a victim to it.

And while I, at 31, was still the same young girl whose mother trained her to be fearful of the nighttime, I was ready to stop running. STORM, with his ridiculous hat and absurd business card, did know me. I had the power to be happy if I wanted to be, and the worst part about realizing that meant I could have been happy the entire time. Happiness was always within reach, I just couldn't see it.

I looked over at Ben, who was sprawled over the whole bed, his big feet poking out underneath the comforter and hanging over the mattress edge, where a plate covered in rice cake crumbs sat on the floor. It was hard packing all six feet five inches of Ben neatly into bed. There were always limbs flying in my face and sheets braided into tight knots, and by morning, if I did manage to fall asleep, I'd usually wake to the sounds of him snoring, curled up sideways in a pretzel with an elbow digging into my ribs. He was a disaster to share a bed with, but seeing him sleep peacefully, especially on that night, made my heart feel full. I smiled at him and bent over to lightly kiss his forehead.

"Muah," I said as my lips grazed his head.

"Uhhhhhh," he whined, swatting me away.

～～～～～～～

Later that month we were in Santa Monica, visiting my parents for the first time since I moved back to California. It was thrilling to be able to get into Ben's car and just drive south to see them, as opposed to the onerous flying routine I'd become used to.

Their house looked the same. Big, white, and stark on the outside, with an absolutely horrific display of Christmas décor inside. A trio of wooden reindeer with bodies made of poinsettias greeted Ben and me as we walked in and gave my parents hugs.

To the left, every inch of the living room was taken over by ceramic carolers, three-feet high and ripe for a Wes Anderson film. Plaid stuffed ducks sat on the couch where the pillows used to be, and in the center of the chaos stood the tree, plastic and yet gorgeous.

"You know we had to do fake again. Real ones can burn the house down," Mom reminded us as she suffocated us in hugs and kisses at the doorway.

Once settled, Mom asked me if I wanted to take a drive with her to Bloomingdale's.

"There's a Bloomingdale's at the mall now?" I asked.

"Yup. There are a couple of things I still need to get and

I just don't trust that they'll arrive on time if I order them online," she explained.

I agreed, excited to be back home. Ben was happy hanging out at their house checking emails and doing work, so I walked outside with Mom and we got into her car.

"Why don't you drive?" she asked, heading for the passenger side.

We made a right on our street, went five blocks south, made another right, went all the way to 4th Street, and turned left, where I cruised toward Bloomingdale's. I was on autopilot. I could do that drive with my eyes closed.

"You still make such good stops," Mom said as I slowed down at a red light. "Always so smooth, like I taught you."

I rolled my eyes and turned up the radio a few more notches.

Once on 4th Street Mom told me which parking structure I had to pull into, and which of the entrances of that parking structure would yield the best result.

"All the stupid women with their yoga mats use the other entrance because it's closer to the studio. God forbid they have to walk and get exercise."

"Still hating those yoga ladies, huh? They haven't turned you?" I asked to annoy her.

"They are so entitled. They swing their mats around intentionally in the market so that I know they are there. So that I know they just came from yoga. They can't leave their mat in the car, they have to carry it like a purse?"

We both laughed.

Mom was right about the parking lot. The entrance we used felt like a VIP entrance and we quickly found a parking spot deep in the opposite corner of the mall.

We got out of the car.

"Here, hand me the keys," she said, extending her arm out to me and fiddling to keep her purse tight against her body.

I looked down at my hand. Mom's key ring was as enormous as ever, dangling with membership cards from practically every market in Santa Monica. Ralph's. Pavilions. Some shoe store I had never heard of. The edges were all peeling. There was a chain connected to a chain that was connected to a long leather key fob. And then there it was, the pièce de résistance: a small hot pink canister of pepper spray. I hated the fact that it was hot pink. Like pepper spray manufacturers had to now pander to women by painting the bottle pink because some algorithm told them that's our favorite color when we're getting attacked?

I knew exactly why Mom wanted the keys, but something inside of me wouldn't budge. I didn't want to give her the satisfaction. Holding those ridiculous keys firmly in her hand was her safety blanket. The 100 or so yards we'd have to walk to get to the stairwell was going to put her on edge, and the keys were going to make her feel in control. And for the first time I just didn't want to participate in it. While I knew that one defiant act would never unbind her from her own anxieties and nutty behaviors, I felt like stirring the pot.

"I can't believe you bought a hot pink can of pepper spray," I said, ignoring her request. "They didn't have regular colors?"

"Honey, hand me the keys," she said again.

I opened up my purse, dropped them inside, and zipped it shut, smiling back at her devilishly.

"You are such a brat," she said sweetly, smiling. Mom softly pinched my elbow and kissed me through the air.

Then, we walked together, against the odds, through the parking lot and a sea of potential danger, protected by nothing. Ready to be robbed.

"I love when you are home," she said.

"Same."

CVS, 2014

"I'm going to CVS. Do you need anything?" I asked Ben one Saturday afternoon.

It was January, roughly five months after I moved to be with him in California. He was sitting on a navy blue West Elm couch we'd purchased through Craigslist earlier that month. It was handsome. They both were.

He stopped typing and looked up at me from his laptop.

"Maybe. What are you getting at CVS?"

"Nothing, really. I want to change the address on my prescription. It's wrong. It still says East 3rd Street."

I always made sure I had a full prescription of Ativan on hand. I rarely used it and would never abuse it, but I needed that bottle to be fully stocked. Ativan was my security blanket.

"That sounds like a terrible waste of time," he said. "Who cares if it's wrong, the address doesn't even matter as long as the prescription is right."

It didn't. As long as you were who the bottle said you were

and had the birthdate to prove it, the prescription was yours. I could have lived in a tent by the river for all the CVS pharmacists cared.

"Yeah, I know," I said.

He picked his laptop back up. "Man, you couldn't pay me to spend my Saturday at CVS."

"Alright so I guess you don't need anything," I said sarcastically.

He laughed.

CVS was four blocks from our apartment in Palo Alto. There was plenty of parking in the suburban neighborhood in which we'd chosen to live, but I could never give up the freeing feeling of shutting my door and just walking. Ben had taken me out of New York and dropped me dead center in the 'burbs, but I wasn't about to give up everything.

I stuck earbuds into my ears, selected Cults on my Pandora station, and headed for the CVS wasteland.

Just as Ben said there would be, there was a huge line at the pharmacy that snaked all the way to the entrance. I sighed and got behind the last person. The woman in front of me had a deep, chunky cough. She was most certainly there to pick up an antibiotic, and I was almost certainly going to catch whatever infectious superbug she was disseminating through the air. I flipped my hair over my nose and mouth to act as a germ filter and waited.

"Picking up?" the pharmacist asked when I eventually

got to the counter. His fingers hovered over his keyboard, waiting for me to serve him with my last name.

"Oh, no," I said. "I want to change the address you have for me on file."

He looked up from his computer, disoriented. Like I'd asked him for a green salad. "You can do that over the phone or at CVS.com."

"I tried already," I told him. "It's still wrong on my prescription."

The pharmacist peered over my shoulder at the growing line behind me, then looked at me. "Um," he paused. "Okay."

I gave him my name.

He searched the database on his computer.

"Do you still live in New York?"

"I do not." I smiled at him, chest wide and full of air.

The entire process took less than a minute and when we were finished I asked him for proof. Maybe a confirmation number that suggested that my move was official. There was no going back to the comfort of New York now that CVS was involved.

It didn't need to be signed by a notary, but I had made it official by updating the label on my anti-anxiety medication.

"No, there's no confirmation number," he said. "You're done."

He'd updated my information in the computer and that was all that was required.

How can this be? I thought. I needed something tangible to mark the enormity of the occasion. Here I was in Palo Alto, California, a place I never thought I'd find the strength to go. A city I thought anxiety would keep me from getting to.

I was happy, in a great place with Mom, beyond thrilled to be living with Ben again. This was my moment.

My graduation.

I was no longer the scared little girl that panicked whenever her mom was in another room. I was now the functioning 31-year-old in therapy, making decisions and following through with them.

I'm a fucking happy person, CVS. I envisioned what would happen if I shouted that and pounded my fists on the counter.

I scanned the immediate area for paper to at least get the pharmacist's signature. If he could sign something, I could hang it up on the fridge as a reminder of how far I'd come.

How much I'd achieved.

My Bachelor of Anxiety degree could shine proudly on the refrigerator, with the pharmacist's name impressively scribbled at the bottom.

But the counter was completely bare except for a jug of lime hand sanitizer and a display box of beige compression stockings being sold in packs of three.

"I'll buy this, then," I said, picking up the stockings. "And I'd like a receipt."

51225683R00172

Made in the USA
San Bernardino, CA
16 July 2017